365 Days of Inspirational Messages

A Daily Dose of Thoughtful Reflections

By
M. Eugene Morgan

Edited
by

Joseph D. Ramsey

Published by

Nagrome, LLC

Nagrome, LLC

1151 Freeport Road
Suite #369
Pittsburgh, PA 15238
meu_mor@msn.com
Web: www.ChangeForHealth.com

365 Days of Inspirational Messages

ISBN 978-0-9916191-2-2

Table of Contents

Acknowledgement	iv
Preface	v
January	1
February	33
March	63
April	95
May	127
June	159
July	191
August	223
September	255
October	287
November	319
December	351
References	383
About the Author	427

Acknowledgement

$\mathcal{I}$ would like to thank websites <u>tinybud-dha.com</u>, <u>goodreads.com</u>, and <u>brainyquotes.com</u> for the majority of the quotes that are in this book I've collected in assisting me in searching for the perfect quotes that are aligned with my understanding of change.

Preface

*T*his book; 365 Days of Inspirational Messages: A Daily Dose of Thoughtful Reflections was born out of the Volume I and Volume II Change For Health series which are an accumulation of blog posts from my website www.changeforhealth.com. With this new book I've also hand picked 365 posts from the website to create a year of daily messages to inspire, to evoke new thinking, to challenge to do, to focus on goals, and to get through each day.

The 365 Days of Inspirational Messages are inspired by the work of Dr. Milton Erickson which includes famous quotes from others that ties in his work. I also wrote my own commentaries and reflections on each quote. You will find as you read through this book that not every message come with a quote, however; every quote does come with a message.

January 1

Today Is a New Day and a New Year

*T*oday is a new day and a new year. Today is the time to start our new beginnings. We start from the beginning again. We build on our previous experiences. We can only hope that we made the best decisions last year so that we can have a better foundation to stand on.

We stand today because we made it to a new year. We're grateful that we can start meeting the new goals that we set for ourselves this year. We all hope that this year will be a better year for us. But we must face the reality that we will have challenges ahead. Challenges that are inevitable allow us to rise to the occasion. Sometimes we will fail and sometimes we will succeed, sometimes we will cry, and sometimes we will laugh. Sometimes we will worry and sometimes we will have a peaceful mind.

January 2

Open Minds Open Doors

> "Open minds lead to open doors."
> — Unknown[1]

*A*n open mind is destined to open doors. Opportunities awake us when we're ready, to take them on today. An open mind widens our world; we see things we've hadn't seen before. Also, it helps to have our minds open when it comes to exploring new things. On the other hand, our biases can close doors.

How can we expect to see opportunities when we can't see what's on the other side of the door? Think of us riding in a hot air balloon. Just as we're carried up in a hot air balloon to the sky, when we look down we can see everything.

A closed mind isn't like this; it sees no opportunities. It cannot see beyond the biases. It is not easy for all of us to give up some of our biases. We need to break up some of our prejudices to build new associations and distinctions to help us increase our horizons and expand our world.

Self-Worth or, Possessions

"Your worth consists in what you are and not in what you have." —Thomas A. Edison[2]

*T*homas Edison is making a distinction between what we are and what we have. But the possessions we have are the result of what we are. Therefore, what we do is an expression of what we are. That is, we earn what we have by what we do. And there is no such thing as a free lunch, because, we have to earn our way through merit. So we have to make our way through the world by doing.

We can't take everything we possess everywhere, but we can take our abilities everywhere we go. And our self-worth is where we will find our self-confidence. Self-reliance is where we build confidence that is where our treasure lies. Things are not where we find our self-worth.

January 4

A Lesson Learned

"Though nobody can go back and make a new beginning… Anyone can start over and make a new ending." — Chico Xavier[3]

*W*e go through life learning lessons or we can take our experiences as lessons. If we carefully examined our lives, we then would find that there is a theme. The theme in our lives usually stems from how we grew up and are raised. If we have a re-occurring theme, then we're still learning, or we haven't learned what we are supposed to have learned. We held on to a belief that's been out of date, a belief that needs to be updated.

It's nice to have insight into the 'why"; however, it is better to learn the 'what' because we can develop a plan that can be useful for a change. Although the 'why' can give us insight, the 'what' is more concrete and accessible to grab and hold.

January 5

Small Steps to Success

"Success will never be a big step in the future; success is a small step taken just now." — Jonatan Martensson[4]

It is easier to look at the endgame than to see what we can do now to get to our endgame. Success may be far into the future, however, just talking about it won't get us there. The steps may be difficult, and they are many, but it starts with one step toward our goal. We just have to make our actions consistent, persistent, and keep focused.

When we keep our focus on one thing at a time, we will more likely complete it. It takes time and effort to learn how to maintain the focus on a new thing. If we execute our steps around the same time and place, we begin to develop a pattern or a habit. The habit becomes automatic which keeps away distractions. We do A, B, and C, and then we're done and resume our daily lives and responsibilities.

January 6

Communication and Understanding

"The biggest communication problem is we do not listen to understand. We listen to reply." — Zig Ziglar[5]

Communication is exchanging ideas with one another. When we communicate with one another, we lessen the problem of misunderstanding. Communication helps us to build trust and respect. Listening is an art. We learn a lot about another person if we do more listening. We learn about their likes and dislikes. By listening, we learn about what they're thinking. We learn about how they're thinking.

A speaker paints a rendition of the world to a listener. We want to be listened to, however, and out of respect, we take turns speaking and listening. We need to listen to one another for us to understand. Communication is not a one-sided conversation. However, both parties are in on the speaking and the listening. We all have needs we got to meet, and we address these needs through our communication. Although we communicate with each other, we also communicate with ourselves.

6

January 7

Doing Our Best Today

"The best preparation for tomorrow is today."
— H. Jackson Brown, Jr.[6]

*T*oday ought to be the most important day because our future depends on it. Since we only have today to spend our time in, then it is important to plan one or two things we know we should do to alter our future. If we have some anxiety about tomorrow or our future, then it means that we haven't been doing anything today to change it or prepare for it. If we prepare today, then we will be ready for tomorrow.

We can't predict or alter our future, but we can alter ourselves for the future. Anything could happen between now and our future. Tomorrow starts with our future. Even six hours from now is in the future. So the future doesn't have to be very far away. However, how we spend our time now will determine how well we adjust to that future.

January 8

Run the Day

"Either you run the day or the day runs you."
— Jim Rohn[7]

*W*e have a choice to either run our day or
allow the day to run us. Procrastination is
one example where we allow the day to run us.
Instead of initiating, planning, and executing the
plan promptly, we procrastinate and wait until
we're forced to make a move under the pressure
of a deadline to get things done. When we do
get things done under this kind of pressure, we
experience relief or relief from the pressure. That
relief reinforces the procrastinating behavior, in
which, encourages more procrastination.

In other words, procrastinating behavior
is rewarded by the relief of tension and release
of pressure we put on ourselves. Procrastination
creates an unnecessary burden on ourselves
when we dread doing a task. However, initiating a plan is imperative for running our daily
lives which means taking control of our lives.
When we do more initiating, we gain more self-
respect.

January 9

Enjoy the Scenery

"A truly happy person is one who can enjoy the scenery while on a detour." — Unknown[8]

*I*n other words, our happiness doesn't have to be based on the conveniences of life. When we have to take another route or a detour, we might as well enjoy the trip. We might find and learn something interesting that we hadn't seen before or didn't know existed there.

Life doesn't have to be a routine. It is all right to pull off the road sometimes and just experience the world around us. Looking at and enjoying new sceneries create new meanings and new associations in our minds. So we can often look back and to re-experience those moments.

January 10

Testing Fear

"Fear is faith that it won't work out."
— Unknown[9]

Fear must be tested before we consider it to be true. Fear can keep away from what's real and keeps us in our heads. We need to experience action to get through our unknowns. We can prepare ourselves, and we can anticipate or go through scenarios in our heads over and over, but we still have to act. The action is the most direct way to deal with our fears. Action can help us find out things we didn't know before. We can only study for so long before we eventually have to take some action for us to learn something. Learning by our actions can quickly reduce our fears. What we will discover is fine-tuning our steps to make our situation better.

January 11

Without Flaws

"I have too many flaws to be perfect, but I have
too many blessings to be ungrateful."
— Unknown[10]

*N*o one is without flaws. It is a matter of knowing that we have to live with our flaws and not allowing ourselves to focus too much on them. Instead, we can focus on what we do have available to make our lives better and not use our flaws as an excuse not to live a better life. Life will never be how we think it should be. There is no need to continue fighting what is not a reality but a fantasy we want real. We're meant to use what we already have available for us to learn how to manage life!

January 12

Life's Mysteries

> "Mystery creates wonder and wonder is the
> basis of man's desire to understand."
> — Neil Armstrong[11]

*L*ife is a mystery. There are mysteries all around us to discover. We will only uncover a few in our lifetime. Life would be boring if we know nothing about life. We need to have mystery stimulate our desire to understand things about ourselves and others.

Getting an understanding helps us to be more respectful of life and others. We don't need to know everything about life but to discover things through our life experiences. We just need enough understanding to satisfy our desire. The world is vast, and we only know a fraction, and that's okay. It lets us continue to wonder about the mysteries of life.

January 13

We Do or Fail to Do

"Do not give your attention to what others do
or fail to do; give it to what you do or fail to
do."
— Dhammapada[12]

When we give our attention to what others do or fail to do, we neglect to focus our attention on what we do or fail to do. There are some things we do that will not be enough or we do the wrong things expecting results. And of course, there are things we fail to do because we just don't want to do them. There are things we must do if we want to succeed. It is easier to think of things to do than to do them. Thinking about doing something is just a delay. Effort takes time, energy, and most of all patience when we are in the learning-how-to stages. Some learnings are dry but necessary and some are stimulating.

January 14

The Smallest Deeds

"The smallest deed is better than the greatest intention."— John Burroughs[13]

*I*t is so easy to say that we want to do great things in our lives. It is also easy to feel overwhelmed with anxiety to expect to do great things but only to be left with great intentions. Our egos think that for us to feel good about ourselves we ought to do grandiose things in our lives. But if we start slowly accomplishing small deeds, then we will have continuity to accomplish bigger deeds. Because by the time we get from accomplishing the smallest deeds to accomplishing the biggest deeds, we would have gain genuine confidence, experience, and maturity. Therefore, we will be ready to handle the big deeds in our lives. It is all right to settle for small deeds. Small deeds can be like seeds. They will continue to grow long after the deeds are done, and as long as they are properly planted in enriched soil, with plenty of sunshine, and water.

January 15

Remake Ourselves

"Our greatness lies not so much in being able to remake the world as being able to remake ourselves."— Mahatma Gandhi[14]

*I*f we continuously allow ourselves to be affected by unpleasant events that we can't control, then it is time for an internal change. This is not to imply that we're giving up on changing the world but instead by changing the world we first start with ourselves.

Although we can't force change on someone else, this is not to imply that we should force change on ourselves. Changing ourselves should be made gradually for it to last. Change is a process that shouldn't be rushed but nurtured through stages. Changing means also learning to adapt to new surroundings. We ought not to hold on to the beliefs that everything should stay as they are while everything else is changing.

January 16

Going Beyond Our Limitations

"Once we accept our limits, we go beyond them."— Albert Einstein[15]

*T*his quote above demonstrates that acceptance can be very powerful, instead of thinking that we're the only ones with a limitation or limitations. Everyone we know has limitations especially the people we look up to for guidance. When we hide our limitations from others, we're hiding our limitations from ourselves. Therefore, we haven't accepted the fact that we have them and we must deal with them as they present themselves in our lives.

We carry our limitations everywhere we go so they're a constant reminder. We don't have to see our limitations as dead ends but we can see them as milestones that we have reached or obtained. In other words, our focus shouldn't be on our limitations, but instead on what can we do to achieve our goals. Our limitations are just part of us, they don't have to define us.

January 17

Our Feelings, Our Emotions, Our Thoughts

*W*hen it comes to emotions, patience is required of us. Sometimes it is hard to control how we feel about things. Feelings tell us what we're thinking at the moment. It is easy to compartmentalized our thoughts from what we feel. It is not easy to trace what thoughts we were saying to ourselves to what emotions we feel. However, our thoughts don't necessarily have to be traced.

What we can do is to feel our feelings and, if we need to express our feelings, do so—but also to own our feelings. We're not responsible for what we feel, but we're ultimately responsible for how we use our feelings. We can't allow our feelings to run us but we do need to allow ourselves to emote our feelings appropriately because that's the natural order of things.

January 18

The Right Use of Knowledge

> "Wisdom is the right use of knowledge."
> — Charles H. Spurgeon[16]

*A*lthough acquiring knowledge is a good start to understanding wisdom, we won't get a true understanding until we apply our knowledge to everyday life. The right use of knowledge comes with experience and understanding. Experience and understanding are the hallmarks of wisdom.

We can share our understanding with others, but everyone has to discover for themselves through experiences to find their understanding of life. No one can take away our experiences, because they become part of us. Our experiences live with us forever. Our experiences make us what we're today.

January 19

Reflection of Our Experiences

"If it's still in your mind, it is worth taking the risk." — Paulo Coelho[17]

*W*e all can imagine something we want to make real in our lives. Imagination is very powerful because we can rehearse as many ways possible in our minds how we want something. Imagination allows us to recreate things in our minds without judgment. Imagination allows us to take risks first in our minds before we risk making the idea real. Imagination is a gift that everyone has who is human. Imagination is a reflection of our experiences. It is the visual memory, spatial skills, motor skills, and other senses that we have re-experienced in our imagination and our dreams.

January 20

Let Go and See What Happens

"You don't always need a plan. Sometimes you
just need to breathe, trust, let go, and see what
happens."— Mandy Hale[18]

A plan is desirable when we need structure. However, too much structure can
repress our creativity and our spontaneity. It is
all right to rely on a feeling or our intuition and
to play things out to see where they can lead us.
It is about allowing ourselves to express our creativity externally without being affected by our
rigidity and biases. Creativity allows us to be
free and to be free to let go. This allows our unconscious mind to surface a little and to spill
some new understandings over to our conscious
mind.

We've all experienced saying to ourselves, "Why didn't we think of that?" but we
did, we just didn't think of that right away because when we stop looking for an answer, our
unconscious mind continues searching until a
satisfying answer pops into our head. What a
lovely treat when an idea or a light goes off in
our heads when we least expect it.

January 21

Take the Rest As It Happens

"Make the best use of what is in your power and take the rest as it happens."— Epictetus[19]

*T*hat which is within our power to use, we should use it, or we're giving our power away to circumstances. We don't have to wait for circumstances to force our hand. Instead, we can use the force of our hand to make things happen in the circumstances. We may not have full control over the circumstances, but we can make the best use of control to steer us in the right direction. We take a bit of circumstance as it happens because we need to know more if we want to learn how to get around the situation if it's all possible and if it's necessary for our well-being.

We all want to feel in control all the time, however, that's impossible, which means we need to trust the universe and ourselves. Once we trust and rely on the universe and ourselves, we relinquish some control and we feel freer.

January 22

When We Feel Awkward

"You can only grow if you're willing to feel awkward and uncomfortable when you try something new."— Brian Tracy[20]

*W*hen we feel awkward or uncomfortable, we're experiencing vulnerability. We experience this vulnerability because we feel set up for an attack. We want everyone to see us doing something perfectly.

But for us to learn we have to go through the awkwardness and uncomfortable feelings. And if we practice doing the new thing, we will improve and we will feel confident in our abilities.

We all experienced wanting to give up during this phase of awkwardness and uncomfortable feelings. But those feelings will dissipate as long as we continue to improve on our goals. The struggle is always part of the process of learning a new thing. It's really about how we push through despite our self-defeat thoughts and the critics.

January 23

Strength Grows

"Our strength grows out of our weaknesses."
— Ralph Waldo Emerson[21]

*T*he quote above sounds so profound. It is like a paradox. This quote becomes a riddle when we turn it into a question, "how does our strength grow out of our weaknesses?" Then we found ourselves looking back at our experiences and we say to ourselves "aha!" First of all, there is a certain maturity level we have to experience before we can get an understanding that we do have weaknesses. And to know that we don't have to allow our weaknesses to stop us from meeting our goals. After we acknowledge our weaknesses, we learn to compensate or to use other areas. In other words, we are forced to use other talents as we built our strength by determination, and as well as building our character.

January 24

See the Good in Others

**"When you choose to see the good in others,
you end up finding the good in yourself."
— Unknown[22]**

*W*e can see the good in others if we look
for it. It's easy to see the bad in others if
we disagree with them or if they look different
than us in some way. When we do find the bad
in others, we develop a preconceived idea about
them. We only see a skewed dimension of that
person and not seeing the whole person.

If we see only the bad in others then we
will only see that in ourselves. Instead, we can
accept both the bad and good in others just as
we can accept those things in ourselves. It is a
choice for us to make. Accepting the bad and the
good in others helps us keep our expectation in
neutral.

January 25

On Loving Yourself

"Focus on loving yourself instead of loving the idea of other people loving you."— Unknown[23]

*W*e so much want approval from another person that we forget that we are a person. How come we think that having self-approval is not enough? It only takes one person to believe in us and that makes a world of difference and that one person is the person we see every day in the mirror. We know what we're capable of doing and we have dreams about doing greater things with our lives. If we feel a need to always be the center of attention, then we haven't been self-loving. We haven't accepted ourselves yet. We aren't satisfied with ourselves.

If we can accept and love others, then we can accept and love ourselves and allow others to love us. If we continue to need constant reminders that another loves us, then it's time to remind ourselves to love ourselves. And then we will know for sure how much love we have for others and ourselves.

January 26

Good Intentions

"The best way to keep good intentions from dying is to execute them."— Unknown[24]

*H*aving good intentions is like moving aimlessly without direction. Good intentions are only that— intentions. Good intentions are just thoughts in our heads. Good intentions are only to make the person who's making them feel good about his or her self at first, but, to later experience disappointment. However, if we execute our intentions, then we will experience confidence in ourselves.

There is a certain expectation from others that we will follow through with our intentions. There is something about expressing our intentions publicly that motivates us to want to execute them no matter how difficult it may bring because most of us don't want to let anyone down. That's one of the worse feelings to experience. We want others to have confidence in us and to know that others can rely on us again for future endeavors.

January 27

Don't Be Afraid to Live

"Don't be afraid of death; be afraid of an unlived life. You don't have to live forever; you just have to live."— Natalie Babbitt[25]

Sometimes we get afraid of death not so much because of the unknown but because of the unknown of living. Death is part of the natural order of things and so is life. So since we are alive today, we have now the opportunity to live. Sometimes we get afraid of death not so much because we can't take things with us when we die but because of not making good with our friends and family. Sometimes we get afraid of death not so much because we didn't do everything we wanted to do but because we didn't do the one thing that would have made a difference in the life of another. Sometimes we get afraid of death not so much because we didn't tell enough stories about our life adventures but because of not being there enough as a listener.

January 28

Love Is Love

"The most important thing in this world is to learn to give out love and let it come in."
— Morrie Schwartz[26]

*L*ove accepts self and then others. Love grabs our attention, especially our hearts. Love allows others in our hearts. Love welcomes. Love is blind. Love accepts those who are ignored. Love teaches us how to love. Love brings individuals closer. Love is friendship. Love is transparent. Love is peace. Love is tranquil. Love is not enough. Love conquers all. Love shows its weaknesses. Love strengthens.

Love overcome obstacles. Love wins. Love loses. Love sacrifices. Love gives with all its heart. Love is everywhere if we look for it. Love has a story to tell. Love knows what's in the heart. Love sees all. Love runs deep. Love respects. Love will prevail in the end. Love is never tired. It starts with love. Love lives in us. Love carries on. Love is love.

January 29

Conquering the Self

"It is not the mountain we conquer but ourselves."— Sir Edmund Hillary[27]

his is a very powerful message for us to understand. It is not easy for us to stay focus on a goal. Distractions are inevitable when it comes to staying on track with our goals. There are some days that we don't want to do the work. There are days we have to push ourselves to do the work when we don't feel like it. We've got to be consistent and maintain the work we do so we can reach our goals and that's not always easy to do. Discipline is the key. If we want something bad enough, then we will plow through the delays, the rejections, the criticisms, and disappointments, and all other obstacles. And when we're on the other side of victory, we can be proud of ourselves that we reached our goals on our own.

January 30

A Community of People

"How far we travel in life matters far less than those we meet along the way."— Unknown[28]

*W*hen we highlight our moments, we usually recall the people who touched our lives the most. We have traces of people over the years who have made an impression and we have made a good impression on them. If we look on Facebook, we will see a timeline of photos of our past, which include pictures of people. It could be our family members or our co-workers or it could be friends that we hang out with.

We're a community of people. Most of us enjoy hanging out with other people on special occasions like a birthday party, a celebration, or an award dinner. We participate in holidays together.

Food is the best thing to bring people together. We enjoy sharing a feast, or just simply ordering out lunch together. Friendship is very important to most people because we want to hang out with someone more like us with similar interests.

January 31

Find Ways

*"When you believe something can be done,
really believe, your mind will find ways to do
it."*
— Dr. David Schwartz[29]

The mind is only instructed to do by belief. If we believe that we can't do something, then we will find ways to sabotage, however, if we know that we can do something, then
we will find ways to do it. Even when we see
difficulties ahead and still believe that we can do
it, our minds will not rest until we carry out our
goal.

Our mind is the most powerful machine
in the universe. We don't know how true this is
yet. We have countless examples that we can
look back on to see how our minds are incredi-
ble. Our minds do amazing things for us that we
take for granted. Communication is the high
mark of intelligence. Planning and then executing is another high mark of intelligence. When
we're able to recall a memory without effort, we
know our mind is working.

February 1

It Is Time to Laugh

*I*t is time to laugh. It is time to laugh at ourselves. It is time to laugh with ourselves and with others. We forget to laugh when we take life so seriously.

Laughter is a release of emotion. We feel so much better after a good laugh. We should practice one good laugh daily. Laughter supports health. It also takes practice to find humor in everyday things and/or situations. Laughing with another helps us to connect better.

It is better to laugh out loud than to hold back a laugh. Laughter is a peculiar thing we do. Laughing is spontaneous behavior. Laughing seems like the one emotion that keeps all other emotions in balance. Laughing is a process of breaking up biases. When laughing helps us to break up our biases, we can begin to see things differently.

February 2

He Who Trims Himself

"He who trims himself to suit everyone will soon whittle himself away."— Raymond Hull[30]

We can't please everyone. We will never satisfy everyone because it's impossible. Not everyone is going to like us and we're not going to like everyone. If we want to please someone, then we should be the ones to please ourselves. We can pat ourselves on the back to say well done. We can please others some of the time but not all of the time. And, that's all right to do. Our self-worth isn't about how we please someone but our self-worth is about how we can help others without expecting a return.

That said, we can't ignore people. We get our satisfaction from what we can do for others.

February 3

New Strength and New Thoughts

"With the new day comes new strength and
new thoughts."— Eleanor Roosevelt[31]

*T*oday we have an opportunity to lean on
our strengths because all of us have them.
We use our strengths during the day and renew
our strengths when we retire at night. When we
rise in the morning our strengths are rejuvenat-
ed and so with new thoughts. Our minds are
refreshed and we're ready to go.

We all have different sets of strengths.
We must respect one another strengths as we
respect our own strengths. We all play a part in
this world.

We all have an opportunity to display
our strengths in the work we do each day. We
can feel proud that we have helped someone
today because we leaned on our strengths.

It is nice to feel wanted and have a purposeful life when using our strengths. We know
we're somebody even though we don't feel like
we're somebody sometimes.

February 4

Start Now, Today

> "The secret of getting ahead is getting started."— Mark Twain[32]

*I*f we feel like we're behind, then getting started is the secret to catching up. We stop thinking when we get started and begin learning what we've started. Procrastination is what keeps one from starting something new.

Procrastination is the symptom of self-doubt. We delay progress by doing nothing except think about it, and we don't believe in ourselves to do a good job. However, we must start somewhere or don't start at all. If we're on the verge of deciding, but continue to stay on the fence, then are decisions have already been made.

The decisions that have already been made are ultimately what we don't want to face in our lives. We don't want to admit to ourselves that we decided to not pursue a dream or wish. We don't want to admit this is because we want to keep alive the possibility that we will pursue our dream one of these days. However, the phrase "one of these days," only keeps things open-ended which is hard to pinpoint and continue to stay nonspecific. Instead, let's get off the fence and start now—today.

February 5

Achievement Starts with Desire

> "The starting point of all achievement is desire."
> — Napoleon Hill[33]

*I*f we want it badly enough, then we will achieve it. If we lose sight of our desire, then we will not even start. Desire is our inner drive to succeed. If we could ask ourselves what is the one thing that we could find most desirable? It would be that one thing we know could be life-changing. It's the thing we dream about. It's the thing that preoccupies our thoughts. Our whole being is telling us to go for it. When we decide to go for it, then our fear turns into excitement and desire begins to grow.

We're stronger than we think. As long as we set our minds on something, we desire the most, achievement is just around the corner. We're more than halfway there if the desire is the starting point of all our achievements.

February 6

The World of a Child

"Children are natural Zen masters; their world
is brand new in each and every moment."
— John Bradshaw[34]

*Y*es, children see the world with fresh
eyes. We all can recall our first experiences. Each moment was new to us. We
wanted to touch everything, smell everything,
and taste everything, especially dirt. We were
allowed to play all day long. We didn't have an
agenda; we just enjoy the moments. We didn't
have concept of thinking about tomorrows. We
cried because we were too tired to keep our eyes
opened to experience one more moment of the
day. Then the next morning we crawled into our
parents' bed to only disturb their sleep because
we wanted to play again. We're sitting alone but
not really alone because we're enjoying the
company of an imaginary friend. Everything
around us was big and we were having difficulty reaching for the door knob but somehow we
work around that.

February 7

Prepare Today for Tomorrow's Wants

"It is thrifty to prepare today for the wants of tomorrow." —Aesop[35]

*P*reparation is a form of planning for the future. While we still have our mobility, still have our faculties and our health, it is thrifty to prepare today so we don't have to worry about tomorrow or our future. And yes, we should enjoy life as we make our preparations. Today is a product of all the decisions we've made in our past. We all made good decisions and not so good decisions. We may not get all our wants in life but we do have some in our possessions and we can be thankful today for them.

Our wants aren't necessarily about material things, want can be about relationships, getting involved in a project, spending time on a hobby, participating in a sport involving a team. Preparation can also be about learning something today that we may need later.

February 8

When Inspiration Is a No Show

*W*e get frustrated when inspiration doesn't come when needed. Instead, we must wait until it hit us. When inspiration does hit us, it means our minds are beginning to open up to new ideas. Inspiration stimulates ideas into our minds. If we just keep the inspiration at the forefront of our minds, then we can use it to motivate us enough to make it into something real. It is not always easy for an idea in our heads to become something real, at least something that could be a major change. We need not give up on our inspirations. Maybe there is a reason why we get them. We ought to pay attention and see if they are worth investigating.

February 9

Nature's Pace?

"Adopt the pace of nature: her secret is patience." —Ralph Waldo Emerson[36]

*P*atience is a virtue. Some things take time to learn and then build. Patience is delay gratification. We want results now. We don't want to wait. Patience is the quickest way to reach an outcome in the long run. If we get impatient with ourselves and others, then it's going to take longer than before. Patience is a learned behavior that takes practice. While we wait and see the result of one thing, we can work on the other thing. It is all right to redirect our attention to doing something else. Time seems to move quickly when distracting ourselves with other things.

February 10

Our Story Is Not Over

"One bad chapter doesn't mean your story's over." — Unknown[37]

*W*e all have bad chapters in our lives, and we also have good ones. Not only we are stronger when we go through difficulties, but we also have a better understanding of things than before. Our future selves cannot go back into the past and give our past selves guidance, however, we can give the next generation some guidance. We have regrets; however, we can learn from them. Today it is not too late to re-write our story. Usually, our past is a good indicator of our future. If we don't want to continue this path, we have to alter our present. Altering our present means doing something other than what we've been doing up to now. It is easier to complain than to do something that's out of our comfort zone. However, the more we alter our present, the more we rewrite our story.

February 11

Passionately Curious

> "I have no special talent. I am only passionately curious." — Albert Einstein[38]

*W*e're instinctually curious about the world around us and the world inside us. We're born to want to know about things. Curiosity stimulates the mind, or we stimulated our mind when we ask a question. We want to know the answer to every question we put forth. However, not every question can be answered. And not every question should be replied to until we're ready. The answers may not be as important as we think. When we put forth a question, it means our minds are thinking. We're seeking to expand our thinking, or we weigh the new information against our background and our values. In other words, we interpret the new data based on what's important to us. We do want to see what's behind the door; we want to know how something works. One question is not enough to satisfy our minds. We do want to understand.

February 12

Momentum Builds Confidence

"One way to keep momentum going is to have constantly greater goals." — Michael Korda[39]

*I*t is important to build momentum in what we do because it keeps us on track. Momentum is the energy we need to complete our goals. Why should we stop when we have the momentum, we stop when the energy ceases? Goals are already challenging to meet sometimes. It is nice to have something like momentum pushing us forward and not pulling us back. Each goal we complete builds our self-confidence to handle greater goals. Sure, a higher goal may be a challenge for us to complete but it won't be impossible because we're ready for it. We're ready to complete our next goal as we've learned from completing previous goals. Momentum helps us to keep up the pace we need to achieve our aims.

February 13

When We Make Time

"You will never 'find' time for anything. If you
want time, you must make it."
— Charles Buxton[40]

The quote above is an old cliché, but it is also a truism. It can still apply to our lives especially when we say to ourselves that we don't have the time or enough time to do anything. We can always scale back and prioritize what's important to do first. We forget that we create time. The things we are doing right now is the time we've created. At one point we made a conscious decision to make time to do something and since then it has become an automatic thing we do. When the things we do become automatic, we're no longer in the present. We need to return to the present or step back to see what things we can scale back to create other desirable things we would like to do in our lives.

February 14

The Most Effective Way

"The most effective way to do it, is to do it."
— Amelia Earhart[41]

*I*f we want to get better at something, we have to do it over and over. Doing something once or twice will not cut it. If we do something that makes us uncomfortable enough times, then we will be less uncomfortable. It is all right to get our hands dirty. It's nice to give ourselves room and time to grow. We can only learn so much by watching from the sidelines. Getting into the trenches is the fastest way to learn to do something effectively. Our action is what can move things along. Idleness gets nothing done. Each time we do the new thing, we gain more experiences. We can teach others what we've learned from our experiences.

February 15

Set Goals

"If you aim at nothing, you'll hit it every time."
— Zig Ziglar[42]

*I*t is a time-waster when we don't have a direction in our lives. It is important to aim at something that's in the future so we can do what's necessary today. A goal is something we desire in the end. A goal or aim keeps our minds focused on the task at hand. We can't just wait for something to happen. Instead, we set goals that are obtainable and hope for another day that we have an opportunity to get closer to meeting them. It can be any goal we desire or that we have a passion for doing because that's what's going to make us happy. Goals and obtaining goals can make us happy when we set them and then carry them out. If we desire more control over our lives, then we must set goals and thus meet them.

February 16

In Peace

"You can find peace amidst the storms that threaten you." — Joseph B. Wirthlin[43]

*P*eace comes from within not from external events. We don't need to be in control of external things for us to be peaceful. Sometimes we inadvertently control things and others with our fears. What will bring peace to us is if we surrender to the reality of our situation. Accepting life as it is can bring about peace from within. We're human beings that need to control because we want to protect our vulnerabilities. We don't want to hurt or experience pain. However, the reality is that pain reminds us that we're alive, and that's a good thing. It would be a terrible thing if we couldn't feel pain. We don't have to hide our pain from ourselves but to feel the pain and then eventually we'll experience peace in our minds and hearts as we heal. We will no longer have to feel threatened.

February 17

Designing Your Life Plan

"If you don't design your own life plan,
chances are you'll fall into someone else's plan.
And guess what they have planned for you?
Not much." — Jim Rohn[44]

As adults, it is up to us to design our life
than to let someone else create it for
us. If we see what desires we have in our hearts,
then we should follow them. We ought to find
what path we want to do for the remaining of
our lives. So at the end of our lives, we don't
have to regret what we didn't do in our lives.
We don't have to have somebody else running
our lives, especially if we don't share the same
desires? Each one of us has to find our path and
then to follow to the best of our abilities. We can
leave our trail of happiness and be glad we did
it. We create the plan for ourselves no one can
lead our lives for us. Creating our path is a sign
of wisdom and maturity.

February 18

The Inner Critic

"When there is no enemy within, the enemies outside cannot hurt you." — African proverb[45]

*W*hy are we so concern about critics when we want to do something out of the ordinary? The critics aren't holding us back; it is our inner critic that keeps us from going the extra mile to get where we want to go. When we display our final product for the world to see, we feel vulnerable to criticism. Criticism is inevitable. Again, our concern for criticism from others is just a reflection of our inner critic. Perfectionism is a hallmark for criticism.

However, no one is perfect. We will not always succeed in our first attempts. We get better over time, and once we reach our peak, we can learn to accept it. Mistakes are an opportunity to learn so we can become our best selves.

February 19

Extraordinary Things

"The simple things are also the most extraordinary things, and only the wise can see them." — Paulo Coelho[46]

*I*f we're more present with our lives, we'll begin to see simple things as extraordinary. It is where we place our attention. The simple things in life are extraordinary if we just take the time to look around. It's all right to pause for a moment and see what we've missed. Watching a lovely sunset or a sunrise seems simple, but it's extraordinary to watch and experience. Experiencing the wind blowing against our face and through our hair but not being able to see the wind is extraordinary.

Walking may seem simple, but it is extraordinary because we're made to stand and walk on two's. Talking may seem simple, but it is extraordinary because communication is very complex.

February 20

Contentment

"He who is contented is rich." — Lao Tzu[47]

Society has sold us on the idea that being rich will lead us to contentment. External things are not enough to satisfy us. Sure, we will be comfortable and have some freedom, but we still feel a longing in our hearts. Contentment is an internal experience as a result of understanding that life is more than just seeing how many goodies we can gather. Living a life of contentment is about letting go of those goodies and just being ourselves while living a meaningful life.

We must look inside ourselves and discover what makes us happy. That's where we will find our contentment.

February 21

Doing Your Best

"Excellence isn't being the best; it's doing your best." — Unknown[48]

$\mathcal{I}$f we're trying to be the best, then we're comparing ourselves with others. However, if we're doing our best, we are competing with ourselves and not others. We're more ourselves when we're doing our best. We don't worry what others say about us when we're focusing on how can we make improvements and not on how we can be better than the other person. Instead, we can help each other to improve on our personal best. We will find more satisfying when we set a personal goal and meet them, than if we get overly competitive with another just because we want to win. It's okay to feed our egos sometimes, however, not to the extent where we have to win most things, because if we lose, it would be a big blow to our ego.

February 22

The Courage to Continue

**"Success is not final, failure is not fatal: it is
the courage to continue that counts."
— Winston[49]**

*I*t is the courage to continue that counts
after success and especially when we fail.
With success and failure, we still have to deal
with our vulnerability. We need to be secure in
our skin. Even after success, we still have to
learn to deal with life. We still have to live a life
worth living. Courage is getting through life
difficulties and not giving up on what's important to us. Some days we will have some successes while other days we will have some failures in life. It is the natural course of life.

February 23

We've Done Enough

"Let whatever you do today be enough."
— Unknown[50]

We can only do so much in the day. At the end of a day, we have to tell ourselves that we've done enough, and we have to let it go. We have to let go of our frustration that's been accumulated. We have to let go of our stressors that's been building as well as letting go of our worries because everything will be there the next day. We have done enough. Now it's time to renew our energies. Now it's time to return to a place of peace. It is time to rest. It is all right to relax. We need a re-organization and a re-orientation so we can be effective tomorrow.

February 24

The Seed of Triumph

"Always seek out the seed of triumph in every adversity." — Og Mandino[51]

*W*hile adversity will happen to us, in the midst of it, why not look for something that we can claim triumph. Our dignity can remain with us amid adversity. We don't have to be trampled by adversity. The seed of victory will start to grow when we begin to have an understanding that our adversity is just temporary, and we're beginning to see the ending. Life difficulties can seem like forever. We still have to continue with life which is a sure way of telling ourselves that we're moving passed our adversities. Sometimes we're like a candle in the wind or so it seems.

February 25

You Can't Unless Imagined

"You can't do it unless you can imagine it."
— George Lucas[52]

*I*magination is a very powerful tool to use to help motivate us into doing something. If we imagine ourselves doing something, then there is a possibility that we will start doing it. Visualizing ourselves where we want to be in the future in our mind's eye helps us to substantiate our beliefs about ourselves that we can do it. Life is difficult already, and not everything will be smooth sailing. There will be some storms and some rough winds. If we're willing to put up with the storms and harsh winds, then we can do what we've imagined if we put our minds to it.

February 26

Starting Over

"It's okay to start over. It's okay to rebuild. It's okay to be scared." — Unknown[53]

*W*hen we start over it is like a new beginning and new opportunity to rebuild our lives. It is normal to be scared when we're starting a new chapter in our lives. We don't know what to expect. We don't know how we're going to handle new challenges. In everything we decide to do, there is always a price. There are the pros and cons of everything we do. We just have to weigh them ourselves based on what's important to us. The pros are our rewards while the cons are our challenges. The cons are challenges to help us put things into perspective. Starting over is like being pushed from our nest and forces to flap our winds. It is time to get on our own again.

February 27

When We're Proud

"I still have a long way to go, but I'm already so far from where I used to be, and I'm proud of that." — Unknown[54]

Whatever efforts we've been putting into such as our projects and our goals, we should be proud of ourselves. Sometimes we wish that things would move along quickly because we can't wait to see the result. In the beginning, we have to be a little patient when we're at the beginning stages while our brains are becoming acquainted with everything. It takes time for the new things we're learning to stick. We know this from life experiences that later on in our learnings when everything begins to click. We then look back and wonder why we didn't understand things sooner. We must allow time to show us when we're ready to accept some new understanding.

February 28

Inspiration Breeds Fullness

> "It's lack that gives us inspiration. It's not
> fullness." — Ray Bradbury[55]

*W*hen you lack something we need, find a
way to compensate; find an alternative,
and think outside the box. We use things differently than before. We utilize more of what we
already have. We remove ourselves from a normal context into a whole different context in
search of a new way of thinking. We receive
fullness whenever we encounter inspiration and
not the other way round. Inspiration is the initial
spark of curiosity. Curiosity can lead us to self-
discovery if we allow ourselves to see what we
are and what we can become.

March 1

Lessons, Acceptance & Gratitude

"No regrets, just lessons. No worries, just acceptance. No expectations, just gratitude. Life is too short." — Unknown[56]

*I*f we turn our regrets into lessons, we will learn something of value. If we would lessen our worries, then we would live our lives better. If we would lower our expectations, then we would be happier.

Our regrets can keep us in the past while our worries keep us fearing the future. Our expectations can keep us disappointed in life. Lessons we learn from life will keep things interesting while acceptance will keep us in peace. Our gratitude will keep us focusing on the things that matter the most.

March 2

Accepting the Struggles of Life

"The secret of being happy is accepting where
you are in life and making the most out of
every day." — Unknown[57]

It is better to start with being happy
where we are than to start not accepting
where we're in our lives. Accepting where we
are in life lets us be less resistant to change. We
don't have to fight with ourselves anymore to
find peace. Making the most out of today allows
us to make our life better if we so desire. Life is
bittersweet. It is not always sweet. Life shouldn't
always be sweet. We need some bitterness for us
to appreciate the sweet parts of life.

March 3

Make Tomorrow Today

> "Many fine things can be done in a day if you
> don't always make that day tomorrow."
> — Unknown[58]

*W*hen we procrastinate, we convince ourselves that we still have time to meet our
goals or complete a task. We say to ourselves we
still can put off our goals and our dreams until
tomorrow. However, when morning arrives, we
play this distraction mind game with ourselves
where we get busy with other things while our
goals remain unattended. When we put forth
effort in accomplishing things, although it gets
complicated, we still feel proud of ourselves
when progress is made, each time we work on
our tasks, to help achieve our goals. We feel
proud of ourselves because we went through a
struggle and pulled through. Pulling through
the struggle made our character stronger than
before.

March 4

Start Loving Yourself

"Stop hating yourself for everything you aren't. Start loving yourself for everything that you are." — Unknown[59]

*I*t takes a lot of energy to be what we think we're not. We don't need to be like someone else. We have a unique way of doing things. That's what makes us unique. We just have to be what we're already are. In other words, we just need to be ourselves and not be afraid to be what we already know about ourselves. It takes less energy to be ourselves. It is unfair to compare ourselves with another when we're two different individuals. There is no one the same as us. Even with identical twins, aren't the same, although before you get to know them you might think they are.

We may be able to imitate someone well, but we can play ourselves superbly.

March 5

We Can Try

"You may be disappointed if you fail, but you are doomed if you don't try." — Beverly Sills[60]

*W*e're disappointed because we have a level of expectation in ourselves to succeed. It is natural to have disappointments in our life. Although it is healthy to have some disappointments, it is unhealthy to stay disappointed with ourselves. Instead of spending time lamenting about how we fail, we can learn from our failures. A failure is our opportunity to see how we can learn to make improvements. We learn through trial and error. We find out what works and what doesn't work for us. We all have to find our way and the inner strength to move past our disappointment and use our time on the how and less on the what in life.

March 6

Chance to Change Your Life

"Every new day is another chance to change
your life." — Unknown[61]

C hanging one's life is difficult. Just because
it gets a little tricky to change something
that doesn't mean we should discontinue trying.
Life is a learning curve. Progress can be at a
snail's pace at first but if we start now, then the
more we learn, the faster our growth will dou-
ble. But if we sit and think and not do, then we
all know that nothing will get done. Nothing is
gained by idleness unless we need to rest.

March 7

Wanting to Control

> "Our anxiety does not come from thinking about the future, but from wanting to control it." — Kahlil Gibran[62]

*W*e think if we could control an external event, then our anxiety will cease. We can't anticipate what we think is going to happen to us in the future. The future is unknown. Anxiety is triggered when we don't know because we want to control things. We have a certain level of control over ourselves, and that's where we should place our attention. We don't have to think that we need to control external events for us to control our anxiety. We just have to do the things we have control over that can be constructive to our well-being.

March 8

Grow Where You Are

"Grow where you are planted."— Proverb[63]

*W*herever we are now in our lives, we still can grow. We still can learn from others we work with every day or people we encounter. We can learn from our mistakes as well as from other's mistakes. Sometimes we want to be repotted to another location because we think that we can be enriched by new things, probably temporarily. However, new things will always turn into old things. Novel things lose their newness with us. We can stay where we are because there are always changes that we have to adapt to and learn.about. As long as we get our nutrients from the soil, water to keep the soil in the pot moist and with plenty of sun rays, we will grow nicely.

March 9

Take a Chance

"The only time you run out of chances is when you stop taking them." — Unknown[64]

The more we put ourselves out there, the more chances we have available. We have to promote ourselves for us to be heard. No one will know we're here if we don't speak up. There are those whose personality is outgoing. They won't have any problems self-promoting. However, those whose personality is more internal will still have to put themselves out there. Yes, we will be vulnerable to attacks and criticisms from others. Attacks and criticisms come with the territory. We will not be able to escape them. So, taking a chance comes with a price; just like everything else we do.

March 10

We Are What We Believe

> "We are what we believe we are."
> — C.S. Lewis[65]

*I*f we say we can't do this or that, we are basing this on a belief. If we say we can do this or that, we are basing this on a belief as well. It is easy to make assumptions about ourselves without really testing them out. Even if we have made few failed attempts, we still used that as evidence that we can't do this or that, therefore our beliefs are reinforced. Instead, we could learn from the failed attempts and look for what we're doing wrong but also look for what we're doing correctly. We ought to look for real proof instead of looking for a reason not to make an earnest effort to do this or that in our lives. It is amazing what the mind can believe and act accordingly without hesitation. We can believe in ourselves and the body will follow.

March 11

Limited by Our Vision

"We are limited, not by our abilities, but by our vision." — Unknown[66]

Sometimes we get caught up into thinking it is our abilities or lack of skills that keeps us limited. If we can only imagine ourselves using our abilities, then we can see how far we can go. We have proof from our past that our abilities got us ahead. We just have to be reminded when we cast doubt on ourselves. Sometimes our vision gets to be so narrowed that we can't see beyond our doubts. That's when we have to take action because taking action is the fastest way to dispense doubts from our minds and so our minds can open up for new opportunities to use our abilities.

March 12

Persistently Persist Resistances

I t is better to persist than to give up. As we persist, we begin to find out more about the problem than if we stopped prematurely. Persistence means to hang in there, enough to get what we need out of it, and then we can decide to stop when we have reached satisfactory. Persistence means going through the hard part of a situation and looking back to see how far we've made it through. Persistence is moving forward through resistance.

March 13

Our Own Self-Worth

"Your value doesn't decrease based on someone's inability to see your worth."
—Unknown[67]

However, our value does increase based on our ability to see that we have self-worth. We don't have to look for external approvals for us to know that we're worthy. We're worthy because each one of us is an individual. As unique individuals, every day we have an opportunity to give to society and to bring a unique perspective on things. Once we see ourselves as unique and worthy, then we can see the worth and uniqueness in others. We then have mutual respect for one another's uniqueness. We become more eager to listen to others' unique perspectives than to quickly tell others what we think. It's about learning and widening our scope.

March 14

What's Possible

*W*hat is possible for one person is not the same as what is possible for another. We all see the world differently. It is through our background that we see the world. Our world is modeled through our upbringing.

We each have the propensity towards a certain talent that we developed over time. Not everyone has the same talent. As one person has a knack for doing a certain thing well, she or he will see what's possible. But as for another person without that same talent won't see what's possible. If we only accept what we already have and build on it, then it only matters to us individually what's possible and how we share with others how it affects us personally.

March 15

Create Joy

"Life will bring you pain all by itself. Your responsibility is to create joy."
— Milton Erickson[68]

*P*ain is inevitable whether that's emotional or physical. It is harder to heal emotional pain because we hold the memory of that event that caused us discomfort. Psychological pain heals with time. However, we can create joy. Just as emotional pain, we hold the memory of events that give us joy. It is all right to feel pain, but we ought to allow ourselves to feel and experience joy. We're entitled to experience joy as much as we want to. We know what makes us joyful in life so lets us recreate it.

March 16

Thinking Freely

*T*hinking differently is the key to how we make changes in our lives. We can't use the same mindset and expect a different result. Instead, thinking differently means changing our mindset. When we change to a different mindset, we have a greater opportunity to see that change is possible. It's a new way of thinking that will motivate us to continue our quest for more changes. When we look back on the progress we've have made over time, it increases our confidence. Self-confidence begets more self-confidence; therefore, we will continue to think freely.

March 17

When We're Challenged

*W*hen we are challenged or we challenge ourselves, it may mean that we want to break through our rigid ideas. Being challenged allows us to break free from our restrictions. Being challenged means going beyond our comfort zone. Being challenged means to find out what we are made of. Being challenged is about self-discovery. If we challenge ourselves, there is an opportunity for possibilities. Being challenged implies that there is more latent potential inside us than we know. If we take on the challenge, then growth is inevitable. If we take on the challenge, then learning something is certain.

March 18

A Smile

"Use your smile to change the world; don't let the world change your smile."— Unknown[69]

A smile is so powerful that it can make a person's day better. When we express a smile to another, we also experience a good feeling that everything will be all right. When we smile, we don't have to expect a return smile back. A smile is a state of expression. A smile can alter a person's physiology. A smile can change our mood into a positive one. So, it is true that a smile from another can affect our model of the world. A smile changes us starting from the inside.

March 19

Where We Place Our Attention

"Dwelling on the negative simply contributes to its power."
— Shirley Maclaine[70]

*I*t is all about where we place our attention. Every day we will be challenged by something we dislike or some unpleasant event that may be affecting our lives. There is not a person in the world who's without experiencing difficulties. We're in this together. Some of us have learned how to handle life difficulties better than others. And none of us is perfect; we have all experienced not handling an unpleasant event very well. That's the part we must accept. We don't have to be so hard on ourselves but only to learn and grow as we mature.

March 20

Act or Forget

> "Complaining is silly. Either act or forget."— Stefan Sagmeister[71]

*J*t is so much easier to complain than to act. If we act, there will always be some risks involved. But if we think the risk is too great, then it is better just to forget about it and move on. If we're complaining, it is more likely about the things that happened or the decisions we've made in our past. Those things will be part of us but they don't have to define who we are as people. Instead, those past regrets are only reminders of how we've seen the world at the time. And we can see now how are past decisions affect us today and we can learn from them.

March 21

What Are Memories?

*M*emories are created from our experiences. In other words, our memories are the offspring of our experiences. Memories are very powerful because we can revisit them and experience them again. Some of our memories are very vivid while others are very faint. Our faint memories are the ones we want to recall the most while some of our vivid memories we just want to delete from our minds. Memories can bring up images, emotions, and smells. Our memories are what we are. Our memories are the foundation of our personality. Since our experiences are the offspring of our memories, then our personalities are made from our experiences.

March 22

Tough People or Tough Times

"Tough times never last, but tough people do."— Robert Schuller[72]

*W*hen we're in the midst of a tough time, it feels like an eternity. When we continue to focus on the feeling of that experience, it becomes difficult for us to see that this will end and that we can get through this if we just hang in there a little longer. A permanent decision doesn't have to be based on a temporary feeling. Instead, if we acknowledge our feelings when we do experience tough times, then the feelings are not as overwhelming or feel like we're out of control. To be tough doesn't necessarily mean that to become disheartened. Being tough could mean that we've learned how to react appropriately to the situation.

March 23

Our Beliefs Are Meant to Be Tested

*I*f we see a task as something unpleasant to do, then we will experience the unpleasant feelings. When we start to experience unpleasant feelings about a task, then we might find a way to avoid doing it. We sometimes get caught up in the feelings of unpleasantness of doing the task that we won't even start or have difficulty starting. When we do this, we don't give ourselves a chance to find out if we like or dislike doing it. The unpleasant feeling is based on a belief that something about the task is not worth putting in the time and effort. However, this generalization is false because the unpleasant feeling is not based on reality. That's why it is all right to challenge our generalization to see if it is true.

March 24

Keep Going

"Don't watch the clock; do what it does. Keep going."— Sam Levenson[73]

*T*his quote is a good analogy of how we get ourselves so easily distracted, instead of doing the work we set out to do. When we look at the clock, we're looking to see how much time we have left to start doing something. Sam Levenson is encouraging us to keep going until it is completed. Milton Erickson says completing things is important. We have all experienced feeling good after finally completing a difficult project. Completing things can boost our confidence. Before we start something we need to consider the possibility that some parts of the process will be difficult. Difficulties are just learning how to widen our minds to find another way to get through things.

March 25

Unexpectedly Surprised

*"If you do nothing unexpected, nothing unex-
pected happens."*— Fay Weldon[74]

*I*f we do something unexpectedly, then
different results may happen. The possibility of getting different results is greater than if
we do something unexpectedly. However, if we
do something that's not beyond what we've already been doing, then we will expect the same
result. We're unexpectedly surprised when
something happens that grabs our attention. It's
really about taking a risk by moving beyond our
comfort zone. It's all right to experience discomfort. The discomfort is only temporary until we
begin to feel some comfort and self-confidence.

March 26

Make Good

"Don't make excuses – make good."
— Elbert Hubbard[75]

*W*e all can make up any excuses to justify our inactions. We've been allowed to make good in the lives of others and ourselves. When we do nothing, we lose out on the opportunities to make our own contributions to humanity, and our environment. We're born into a world of wonderment and curiosity. Children are always pushing the boundaries and limitations so that they can experience everything through their senses. As we get older, we lose some of the wonder, curiosity, and interest in learning. We can rekindle our curiosity when we begin to learn new things about life so we can make good in our lives.

March 27

Carry Away Small Stones

"The man who moves a mountain begins by carrying away small stones." — Confucius[76]

*E*verything big started small. When we focus on how difficult and enormous a task is we tend to run the other way or fill our time up with distractions. Instead, the realization is that we can break down an enormous task into smaller more manageable ones. After we have completed a task, we can reward ourselves. We slowly gain confidence in our abilities, which in turn, motivates us to continue completing the next task and so on until all tasks are completed.

March 28

Happiness Is Not Ready Made

"Happiness is not something ready-made. It comes from your own actions."— Dalai Lama[77]

*H*appiness is a state of mind but to get to that state, the action is a requirement. It is through our actions that alter our mood. We shouldn't wait for happiness to happen. Our actions will not always reward us with happiness. Happiness is not always required to live our life. Happiness is only one of the states of emotions that we experience. To make life colorful, we must experience all states of emotion not just only thrive for just one. Happiness is the result of making progress in our personal life. To make progress in one's life requires action, and then, be content and satisfied as we look back on our life, with fewer regrets.

March 29

Break a Record

"Adversity causes some men to break; others to break records." — William Arthur Ward[78]

*W*e all have experienced adversities in our lives. Some of us have experienced more adversities than others. It is hard to cope with adversity alone. But we can band together to help one another, especially, when the same adversity is affecting the other person as well. It is through encouragement that we get our strength to move through it. We don't have to be broken by adversity but see adversity as another opportunity to experience the feeling of pain, anguish, grief, sympathy, loss, comfort, acceptance, and finally the beginning of healing as a community, therefore as an individual. This is how we break through anything.

March 30

Producing Value Is a Purchase

Some of us aren't self-starters. We need someone to push us a little to produce action. If we are a sole person working on a project, it is easy to procrastinate, create distractions. But if we tell another what we're doing and to have it done a specific time, then we feel accountable for completing it. Being accountable is a very good motivator for those of us who aren't self-starters because we don't want to disappoint. Having a good purpose can be another good motivator, especially, if the purpose is about helping others and giving them value or solving a problem. If we can meet the need of another, then we're giving them value.

March 31

An Idea

*A*n idea can change how we look at things. An idea can be powerful when it becomes real. An idea can move a mountain if we let it. An idea is invisible but it can make legs walk and make a mouth talk. An idea can illuminate the dark well. An idea is like a lighthouse, it can help us find our way. An idea is a food for thought. An idea grows as long as we think it. An idea can motivate us into doing something extraordinary if we let it. An idea can recreate a new world. An idea can bring us together in the most powerful way.

April 1

Curiosity and Learning

*C*uriosity is the beginning of learning. Curiosity holds our attention long enough to learn something and remember what we have learned. And learning should be fun. Our neurons in our brain can only take so many dry facts before they get fatigued. Our brain needs constant stimulation, which means we're always looking for novelties to capture our interest, long enough to learn something about them.

For us to learn effectively we must be in an environment where it is safe and learning is encouraged. Fear can zap out our curiosity and without curiosity, it is difficult for us to learn and develop and master a skill. It is all right to enjoy the experience of learning new things and have fun during the experience.

April 2

Right Direction

"If you are facing in the right direction, all you
need to do is keep on walking."
— Gautama Buddha[79]

Sometimes we find ourselves lost in our
distractions that we walk in a circular
fashion because we don't have purpose and/or
goal in mind. Purpose can mean placing meaning into the goals we set for ourselves. Without
a purpose there is no meaning, therefore the
goal is not worth pursuing and without a clear
direction. Our purpose is what we need in order
to constantly remind ourselves why we do
things we do to complete our goals.

April 3

Finding Another Way of Thinking

*F*or us to get around or through a prob-lem, we must find another way of think-ing. If our conclusions are dead ends, then it is time to revamp the way we're thinking about the problem. We need to re-educate ourselves by looking at the problem with a new entry point. This will steer us into a new direction, instead of falling into a trap which leads us to a dead-end in the first place. Although the new entry point could lead us to another dead-end, it's a good technique to help us think in diverse ways rather than think one way.

April 4

When Do We Start

*H*ave we really started on what we set out to do? Or are we still thinking about what are the next steps? How long do we continue thinking about what's the next thing to do? If we just set up an agenda for the week and make it our goal to complete it by the end of the week, then we will have laid a foundation for the next week. When we look back at the end of year, we will see that we have accomplished many things. What we do now will be our foundation for what we build upon tomorrow. Each day is a gift and an opportunity to focus on the present. Tomorrow is only imagined, but today we're in the here and now.

April 5

Plan, Then Execute Intelligently

"The idle mind knows not what it wants."
— Ennius[80]

*I*n other words, the idle mind is day-dreaming and not consciously thinking about what to do next. We ought to deliberately think about our next course of action. Our mind is what moves our body and not our feelings. We've got to make an intelligent plan and then execute without feeling. Feelings usually follow initially after the action has taken place. If we sat idle waiting for a feeling to move us into action, we will be sitting for a long time. That's why it is important to plan and execute intelligently and consciously.

April 6

Ambition Starts with Intelligence

"Intelligence without ambition is a bird without wings." — Salvador Dali[81]

*W*e have to use our intelligence to aid us to get ahead. Ambition cannot do without intelligence while intelligence cannot do without ambition. We need both of them to succeed in life. Just as the bird will indeed die without its wings, we will only be a vegetable without ambition. Dreams feed the mind with learning experiences. There is nothing wrong with ambition as long as we have a moral compass. Ambition is another way of saying we have a desire to meet our goals with determination. A bird needs its wings to find food, to find twigs to build a nest, to find a mate. A bird pretty much does everything with its wings. Therefore, everything we do that requires us to complete tasks is also ambition.

April 7

Don't Stop, Persist

*W*e don't have to stop when things get harder. It is all right to be persistent even if we're alone in our struggle. Being persistent means that we will never give up. We all have seen plants grow through hard soil and even through concrete. The plants were persistent in their growth and were rewarded with light from the sun. We got to be like those plants that grew through concrete and just keep going until we reach a milestone and an opportunity to look back to see that progress was made through our efforts and our struggles.

April 8

Reorientation, Changes Us, Not Things

*I*t is good to get away from the same routine. Traveling a distance is one of the best ways to clear our minds. While we're away from home, we develop a new routine. Developing a new routine requires us to adjust our behaviors to accommodate our new surroundings. With new behaviors, we now have new routines until we return from our travels. In new surroundings, there is a freshness about them where new learnings take place. We have all experienced returning home while things are in the same places, but we experienced freshness about our home. This means that we leave from our travels with a new reorientation and new learnings that we brought back with us. With these new reorientations and learnings, we have an opportunity to continue to stimulate growth.

April 9

Getting Unstuck

*W*hen things aren't going the way, we want them to go, we get frustrated and feel stuck. When we get frustrated and feel stuck, it is time to look inside us for resources to get unstuck. It is time to utilize what we already have for things to start changing. We also need to begin to readjust our behavior to the situation that's getting us frustrated and stuck. We don't have to add to the bad luck with our frustration; it just makes things worse. Instead, we can see what we can do in ourselves to change our attitude and our perception of what's making us frustrated and feel stuck. That's the first start. Then we can alter our behaviors in making small accomplishments until we fulfill our desire.

April 10

Take Control of Your Life

*I*f we can't control what's around us, then let us take control of our own lives. We're pretty much the pilots of our lives. We still have to make the final decision to where we want our lives to go. Even if we look for answers from others or meditate or pray for answers from a higher power or the universe, we still have to make the final decisions about what we think is best for ourselves. Taking charge of one's life could mean fulfilling a dream, going back to college, writing a book, learning a new hobby, going on a trip to a place where we haven't gone before, learning a new language, etc.

April 11

Making Other Lives Better

"Your life will become better by making other lives better." – Will Smith[82]

*I*f the majority of the world's population strove to help another in need, then there would be no such thing as poverty. There would be peace in the world. There would be no hunger. It starts with one person to find ways to make another person's life better. We can start small in making other lives better. It doesn't have to be something big. It depends on what the individual needs are and how we can help that individual or individuals.

April 12

Everything Is Temporary

*W*hen things are going well in our lives, we ought to appreciate every moment because it won't last. But when there are some difficulties in our life, then we can be reminded that the unpleasant experience is only temporary. It is not lasting. Everything has a beginning, middle, and ending. Our difficulties will eventually pass. So if we look at this way, we can better deal with things in our lives if we are not overwhelmed by them. Since everything is constantly changing, there is no such thing is permanency. Getting some perspective on things is very helpful in dealing with life challenges.

April 13

Revisiting Our Motives

Sometimes, we do things so automatically that we forget about our intentions for doing them in the first place or reasoning behind them. It is good to revisit our motivations or reasoning behind our behaviors. If we think the motives of our behaviors are reasonable, then we can continue to do them so long as they are useful and constructive. But if they aren't useful to what we're trying to achieve, then we can discontinue using the behaviors and replace them with something else that is useful. Knowing about our motives of our behaviors can give us a clearer picture and insight into what direction we want to take next. It is good to make adjustments along the way.

April 14

With a Little Encouragement

*G*etting a little encouragement from others goes a long way when we're in a state of self-doubt. Self-doubt has nothing to do with our abilities. Self-doubt is the belief that we can't do what we want to do. When we're in the state of self-doubt, we're looking only at what we're lacking instead of looking at what we can do to learn and grow into what we desire. Being in the state of self-doubt only keeps us away from the many tasks that are required of us for growth to take place. And getting positive reinforcements from others is the difference that makes the difference.

April 15

A Participant or a Sideliner

*W*e don't have to live our lives on the sideline when we're in charge of making our own decisions. Sideline is a time for vicariously watching and learning from others. After a time watching participants, we then begin to model them. But later we begin to claim our sound, our voice by remodeling the way that's uniquely ours. Modeling another is an external process while remodeling is more of an internal process that starts from the inside out. Remodeling allows us to interpret our learning based on our background and our unique view of the world. So, the more we are a participant of this world, the more we become ourselves and uniquely express ourselves to the world.

April 16

Growth and Flexibility

F or us to grow, we must be flexible. For us to be flexible, we must widen our world. There will come a time when we will need to bend a little for us to move forward. Being flexible doesn't mean that we are doormats. It is quite the opposite, being flexible means we're getting stronger. Compromise is part of the process of being flexible; we have to weigh in on the pros and the cons in each situation. When we're flexible we see things we haven't seen before, we have more possibilities and opportunities in our lives.

April 17

Respect Yourself, First

*W*e first have to respect ourselves before we can demand respect from others. If we disrespect ourselves, it would be difficult for us to respect others. If we disrespect others, it would be difficult for others to respect us. Respect is about doing to others what we would like others to do to us. One of the quickest ways to anger another is to be disrespectful. And one of the quickest ways to decrease anger in another is to be respectful. When we make an effort in helping someone, the individual will see that in our actions and know that we're genuine. Respect is known by our actions.

April 18

The Trail We Leave Behind

> "No one saves us but ourselves. No one can and no one may. We ourselves must walk the path." — Gautama Buddha[83]

*N*o matter how much help and advice we get, we ultimately have to save ourselves. We still have to decide alone what we have to do next in our life. We each have our path to walk. And once we discover our path; sometimes it is not easy to walk it. Sometimes it is not easy for everyone to walk one's path. Sometimes, we resist walking the path we know is ours. But if we meet our path with less resistance and embrace it, then maybe our path will be easier to walk. We see our path when we look back at the trail we have left behind.

April 19

Learning Is an Opportunity

*I*f we're not familiar with a subject, then we have an opportunity to learn something about it. No one knows everything. Sure, there will always be someone smarter. But that shouldn't stop us from learning a thing or two about the subject. Because we're done with school doesn't mean we stop learning. Not only is the phrase "knowledge is power" is an old cliché; it is a truism. We can use our learning to be our best unique self. We can use our learning to inspire others to be their best unique self. Learning is an opportunity for personal growth. It is not about how smart a person is; it is about learning to enrich one's life.

April 20

It's Okay to Think About Self

*W*e need to do a bit of thinking for ourselves. We have a storehouse of experiences and understandings that our unconscious mind can sort out for us. Nobody else can do our thinking for us. It is our job to do that for ourselves. Our experiences and understandings are unique to us in that we know what's best for us. Thinking is about learning from our understandings and past experiences. For instance, we can ask ourselves, how can this understanding help me today or what can I learn from past experiences to help with this situation today? This is about self-discovery.

April 21

We Can Make a Difference

"If you think you are too small to make a difference, try sleeping with a mosquito."
— Dalai Lama XIV[84]

*T*his quote from Dalai Lama refers to making a difference to change or to have an effect on the world. This can also be applied to making a difference in one's life. We can effect change if we stand up and believe in the possibility and take advantage of the opportunities when it presents itself. We don't have to just wait for something to happen; instead, we can proactively look for opportunities where others aren't looking. We don't have to be afraid to check things out because not every opportunity is going to be useful but we can find what opportunity will suit our situation.

April 22

Memories in Pictures

$\mathscr{P}$ictures are moments in time and space. We don't want to forget the special occasions that we want to cherish forever. So we capture these moments through pictures, sounds, and smells. And when many years have gone by, we can revisit those moments by thumbing through our photo albums and re-experience those precious moments which were our happiest times and some of our saddest times. Memories are very powerful. Memories can affect us in many ways. A picture can trigger a memory that we haven't recalled in a long time. Memories can induce different emotions that we haven't felt in a long time. Memories can be helpful or they can be hurtful. Some memories we would rather not recall while some we don't want to forget.

April 23

Quiet Sounds

Sometimes we need to get away from noisy and loud sounds. Loud sounds can be overstimulating. It is good to have some silence so we can hear the sound of our breathing. We can hear our intimate thoughts. Quiet sounds can help us to focus inwardly and create peace of mind and can quiet the mind. We're allowed to get back to our rhythm and we can be centered again. A ticking clock can also be soothing to our ears while reading an interesting book. Low sounds can quickly ease us to a nice sound sleep.

April 24

When We Think the Grass Is Greener

*W*hen we think the grass is greener on the other side, then it may mean that we're forgetting or dismissing the things we've worked so hard to get. A desire creates a need to have and want something. Once we fulfill that want or desire, our attention towards it ceases. When we are no longer interested in that want or desire, we move on to the next thing that grabs our attention. Even if we had the greenest grass in our neighborhood the novelty will eventually wear off.

But we can be grateful for what we already have in our lives. We can be grateful for our physical health when others are struggling with their health. We can be grateful for still having a job during the recession. We can be grateful to have water when other parts of the world are without. If we think about it, we can all find something grateful for our lives today.

April 25

Conquered by Self

> "If you do not conquer self, you will be conquered by self." — Napoleon Hill[85]

C hange creates resistance. We all know that change isn't always fun. Change is difficult sometimes. It's a lot easier to find excuses or distractions than to accept the fact that change is inevitable. Conquering self can free us from our self. Our feelings are not a good excuse to do nothing when it is required of us to do something to make a change. We cannot rely on our feelings to get the job done. We have to rely on self-discipline, which means that we do things anyway despite our fears, our doubts, and our uncertainties. It is through our behaviors that we can generate a feeling of confidence and self-respect, which can lower our trepidations.

April 26

Worrying Serves No Purpose

"Worry pretends to be necessary but serves no useful purpose" — Eckhart Tolle[86]

*W*orry can distract us from focusing on the task. Worry keeps us alone in our world. Worry delays progress in our lives. Worry doesn't support health. Worry is just a habit we just do. Worry is a time-waster. Worry can preoccupy our minds with foolish thinking that has nothing to with the specific task. However, if we just do and deal with what's worrying us then we will feel more in control of our lives and not be paralyzed with worrying.

April 27

The Unwritten Future

> "A man with outward courage dares to die; a man with inner courage dares to live."
> — Lao Tzu, Tao Te Ching[87]

*O*ur trepidations about death are really about our trepidations about life. We can be afraid of living the life we want. It takes courage to start on something new that we aren't used to doing. The unknown creates fear. We don't know how things are going to be in the future. The truth is that our future has not been written so whatever the decisions we make can mold our future. We have the power; we've just got to believe. The decisions we've made in our past dictate what we're doing today. If we want to make a change for something else, it is better to carefully consider our decisions today for an unwritten future.

April 28

When Dreams Don't Come True

*N*ot every one of our dreams will come true, this is a reality we must face. All of our dreams aren't meant to come true but some of them will. A dream is our hope to satisfy something in our lives. A dream is something we think about how to get us motivated. A dream is the stuff that makes things real in the future. Dreams let us work things out in our heads before we make them real. A dream helps us to consider the possibility that something can become real. Some of our dreams should remain dreams and not made real.

April 29

A Shift in the Way We Look

Sometimes we've just got to look at a problem differently for us to better handle it. It does us no good to look at the problem the same way but only see it as something we can't manage. Just a shift in the way we look at it can help us see things that seemed at the time impossible to solve. We are able to do; we just have to remove the blinders away from our eyes to see. Things weren't hidden from us; we just didn't know what and where to look. We don't have to look very far for our treasure, because we all possess them. We've just got to learn how to use them.

April 30

A Rock and a Hard Place

*W*hen we're between a rock and a hard place, we find ourselves feeling stuck. When this happens, it is time to wait and see. Things seem to work themselves out if we wait until an opportunity presents itself for us to take. Everything is in constant change; nothing stays the same. We just have to wait until something comes up that will help us get ourselves unstuck and move on with our lives. Opportunity will come knocking at our door, if we're home to answer it.

May 1

Struggle and Strength

"The struggle you're in today is developing the strength you need for tomorrow. Don't give up." — Robert Tew[88]

To struggle doesn't mean we're weak. To struggle means, we're pushing forward despite the difficulty at the moment. It is not always easy to focus when there are distractions. It is not easy to push forward when we don't feel like doing it. It is not easy to take another step when doubting thoughts are swirling inside our heads. It is not easy when there is not enough time to put in the effort. It is especially not easy to strive for better when there are others not supportive and doubting us. However, we must not give up and give in to our weaknesses but build on the strengths and courage that we have acquired over the years.

May 2

The Need to be Appreciated

"The deepest craving of human nature is the need to be appreciated." — Williams James[89]

We all want to feel and be useful in our world. No one wants to feel different than the next person because we want to be a part of something. No one wants to be isolated from a group. We desire to have friends, and we like it when someone calls us by our name. It is human nature to be wanted in any group. Trust is always a factor. Trust is earned. Trust is usually earned when two or more individual handles a difficult situation together because we're forced to rely on each other as a team. Every group is a unit. In the unit, each person has to play a part for the unit to function well. Each member of the group begins to learn about the other's strengths and weaknesses, and each member learns to anticipate the other's needs. We're emotionally linked together.

May 3

You Think You Can

"Whether you think you can or whether you think you can't, you're right." — Henry Ford[90]

*T*he brain only does what we think. If we think we can't do this or that, then our brain will find a way to prove that we can't do this or that. However, if we think we can do this or that thing, then our brain will find a way to prove that we can do this or that thing. When we find a way to prove that we can't do this or that thing, then it means that we have a high expectation that we should be able to do a new thing flawlessly. However, when we find a way to prove that we can do this or that thing, we have an understanding that it will take time and patience to learn the required skills before we become proficient. We learn through trial and error, not through assumptions, to find our way in the world.

May 4

Learning and Growth

*"Develop a passion for learning. If you do, you
will never cease to grow."*
— Anthony J. D'Angelo[91]

*O*ur mind is made for learning new things
every day. It is a gift. Learning is giving
us the ability to grow into what we want
to become. We're at different levels of learning.
Therefore, we're at different levels of growth. We
find our journey through learning. Learning is
about adapting to new surroundings. There are
some things we learn that we need to unlearn,
and there are good lessons we've forgotten that
we have to relearn. We need to be reminded that
once upon a time that our first learnings were
difficult, but we managed and learned what we
needed to learn. Since then we have a storehouse of learnings that have accumulated over
the years through experiences, a treasure chest
of experiences we can always tap into if needed.

May 5

Mistake and Idleness

"A life spent making mistakes is not only more honorable, but more useful than a life spent doing nothing." — George Bernard Shaw[92]

*I*f we make mistakes, then, at least, we have some stories to tell the next generation. We make mistakes for us to learn about ourselves. We won't know much about ourselves if we do nothing with our lives. Making a mistake is what makes us human. When we accept the fact that we make mistakes, then we won't be afraid to take risks. We don't have to take big risks to prove to ourselves that we have courage. It's okay to start with small risks. Learning is about taking risks. Our minds are closed to new things when we're afraid to learn. Someone with an open mind is willing to learn new things. Our level of anxiety decreases when we're informed about something new because we have a new understanding that makes us more aware of things.

May 6

Discipline, Goals and Accomplishments

"Discipline is the bridge between goals and accomplishment." — Jim Rohn[93]

Discipline is about completing every task that will take us to our goals. Discipline has its reward. Discipline allows us to stay focus despite the chaos. Discipline assists us in acquiring good habits. Discipline helps us to hold it together when we need to until we're ready to let it go later. Discipline is difficult, but we're satisfied after completing each task. Discipline is telling us to keep hanging on because we're almost there. Discipline is like a friend we take in or a foe we keep out. It is up to us to embrace discipline because we have it to assist us, not to punish us. Besides, we punish ourselves enough with our doubts. Discipline guarantees consistency with everything we do. Discipline keeps us on track and in order.

May 7

Archetype of a Warrior

*I*t is important to remember those who have left this life. Especially those who have made the last sacrifice for us to experience the freedoms that we hold dear to our hearts. Let us not take for granted our freedoms, instead, honor our lives with them. The way we can honor our lives with our freedoms is to live a warrior's life. The archetype of a warrior is one who plans, set goals, and complete them through discipline and concentration. A warrior is willing to go the extra mile without hesitation. These are the characteristics of the warrior. Every one of us has this archetype within us where we can tap into bringing about those characteristics if we want to do more in our lives.

May 8

Success, a Character Builder

> "Success builds character. Failure reveals it." — Dave Checketts[94]

*I*n other words, how we deal with failure is an indication as to how well we succeed. Our struggle for success is a character builder. We learn to get tougher skin when we struggle. It is just as important to fail as it is to succeed. Success is built upon failures because we continue through the struggles until we get to where we want to go. Struggling is a part of everyday life to help us to learn how to live and interact with the world. Struggling makes us a stronger candidate for success. Struggle helps us to grow into our potential if we don't give up but continue the path that we set for ourselves. It is tough to look at ourselves in the mirror to see what failure reveals to us. We discover the kind of characteristics or traits that are floating to the surface of our psyche. It is really about self-discovery.

May 9

Find Our Talent

"If you don't decide what your life is about, it
defaults to what you spend your days doing."
— Robert Brault[95]

*H*aving a purpose is what makes
things we do meaningful. We need
a purpose in our lives so we can
satisfy a need, desire, or fulfillment. We feed our
souls when we have a purpose. Without a purpose, there is no direction or destiny but what
we may experience is mundane. Each one of us
has been given the gift of life. And with this life,
we've been allowed to celebrate life through our
unique talents. Each one of us has been given
more than one talent, and it's up to us to discover our gifts while we walk our journey of life.

May 10

Life Is to Be Experienced

"Life is not a problem to be solved, but a reality to be experienced." — Soren Kierkegaard[96]

*L*ife isn't supposed to be smooth sailing. How do we learn if we don't experience life as it is? There will always be ups and downs because that's a part of life we can't avoid or solve; we just have to accept that reality. We ought to see life as it is and whatever life brings to us we can use the inner resources that we have accumulated over the years to assist us in getting through difficult times. Besides, we can't fix everything in life. Life usually works itself out in the long run; we can't see this is because we're only here temporarily. We're part of something bigger than what we can imagine. We somehow play a role in this mystery of life. No one has a definitive answer, and we don't need one necessarily because life is about experiencing the world, learning and self-discovering.

May 11

Today's Seed and Tomorrow's Flowers

"All the flowers of all the tomorrows are in the seeds of today." — Proverb[97]

Today we plant seeds in the soil. Tomorrow we water the soil in the pot. We don't expect the seeds to grow flowers in a day. We watched while waiting patiently. We checked the soil for dryness. We imagined how the plant would bloom into a flower. But we only see dirt in a pot. We make sure there is enough sunlight. After a month, we still see nothing but dirt in the pot. We wonder if there is anything more we can do. Should we give it more water or add more soil? However, we forget it takes time for a seed to start growing into a plant and the plant has to grow through thick soil. The plant is growing against thick soil and gravity. This is all happening in the soil. We don't know if this is happening because it's unseen progress. We continue to water because we have an expectation and an image in mind what it would look like. We stay with this image by attending to the pot every day or every other day until the imagined flowers in our mind become real.

May 12

No Burnt Rice

"There is no burnt rice to a hungry person."
—Philippine Proverb[98]

$\mathcal{E}$ verything we see depends on our perspective or the context of the situation. Sometimes we don't understand something but later develop a new perspective when we're ready for new information. Perspective depends on what's important to us and how we proceed with things. What's important this morning will not necessarily be important this evening. Our values oscillate depending on what we need at that moment. What we need at that moment takes precedence over what's less important. Just like the quote, the hungry person didn't care about burnt rice. The hungry person sees no burnt rice, but rice to fill an empty stomach. The hungry person's values have swung to the least important (the burnt rice) until his or her basic needs are fulfilled (hunger).

May 13

Having an Inner Life

"The man who has no inner-life is a slave to his surroundings."— Henri Frederic Amiel[99]

*I*t is easier to get caught up with our surroundings than to stop and sit alone and then close our eyes. We need an inner life for us to maintain a balanced life. It is time to listen to the inner voice that's telling us to slow down. It is time to pay more attention to what our bodies are telling us. It's okay to rest for a moment. Taking breaks between our busy schedules can help renew our bodies and develop a peaceful mind. Having a calm mind can help us to handle our surroundings better. We just have to permit ourselves to relax more and not to take things so seriously. We've only got one life.

May 14

Expect Things

"You have to expect things of yourself before you can do them." — Michael Jordan[100]

The expectation is the push that we need to make things happen. We have to hold ourselves accountable because our nature likes to stray away from our goal. We want to get distracted. So, we have to keep ourselves in check. What keeps us in check is the intellectual part of us that plans ahead and then execute the plan. We can't allow our feelings to dictate our lives. We're rewarded with good feelings when we complete a project. It builds our self-confidence. If we have confidence in ourselves, then others will notice our confidence, and they will respect us for it. The self earns respect by the self. Our confidence will continue to grow as long as we believe that we have the potential to do things if we just keep our minds on the goal.

May 15

When the Student Is Ready

"When the student is ready, the master appears." — Buddhist Proverb[101]

*A*s long as we have a tug of war between our internal parts, we will never be ready. The tug of war is between the part that wants to learn new things and the other part that cautiously wants to stay put and is satisfied. Both parts have to meet somehow in the middle and make a compromise. We can tell our learning part of ourselves to be patient and to take our time learning how to do things. And then tell our cautious part of ourselves to take one step at one time or take small steps. Both parts have to agree to do the same thing for us to move forward and how we should move forward. Once both parts agree, then we're ready to allow life to teach us what we need to know about something. We need both parts for us to function adequately and be present for us to learn from the master of life.

May 16

Curiosity and Achievement

"Curiosity is the engine of achievement."
— Ken Robinson[102]

*C*uriosity is the beginning of learning. We want to know how things work and for what reason they work. As children, after many uses, we break open our toys to see what's inside them, especially the ones that are electronic to understand how they work. It becomes a mystery, and we want the mystery to be solved. Once we see what's inside, we then get some understanding, and some of the mysteries are gone, but we're still amazed at the different parts that created something special. Amazingly, we as humans can create something real out of our imagination. It's like magic. It's like magic because that toy first started as an idea and then an image in someone's head. So, whatever we imagined ourselves to be we become that image.

May 17

Enjoying the Moment

"The best way to pay for a lovely moment is to enjoy it." — Richard Bach[103]

*O*ur moments are for the time we enjoy spending together with friends and family. We create our moments when we're in the present enjoying ourselves. Being in the moment implies that we're not looking back at our past, and we're not worrying about the future. Therefore, we're experiencing joy because we're not blaming our past, and we're not stricken with the anxiety of the future. Experiencing the moment is a time of rest and renewing ourselves again. Living in the moment means we have time to experience life as it is. We have time to process things we've been holding off on. Living in the moment is consciously living instead of doing everything automatically.

May 18

Made to Happen

> "Things do not happen. Things are made to happen." — John F. Kennedy[104]

*I*f we want to do something greater than what we are doing today, then we have to make things happen. We're deliberate when things are made to happen. When our actions are intentional, we're more in control of our lives. We design things and designing is intentional. There is some planning when it comes to creating new things. This is about being proactive instead of being reactive. We can't be proactive and a victim at the same time. If we want to live our life the way we want, then we must be proactive. We have to make decisions based on our values, not on our feelings. We can stop dreaming of a different life. Instead, we can start doing it until we match the prototype of our idea.

May 19

The More We Do

"The more we do, the more we can do."
—William Hazlitt[105]

*I*n other words, first, do what we already can do. The more we do what we already can do, the more confidence we have in ourselves to do more of what we can do. We develop our skills through repetition as well as confidence. Our expertise and trust are built upon each other. These things take time and patience with ourselves to develop. It also takes maturity to know that there are some skills that we're just not good at it and to leave it to those who are good at it. Instead, we can continue to focus on the things we can do and discover new ways of using our gifts to do new things we haven't yet learned how to do. We don't have to stay with the belief that we're only limited to do certain things. Human beings can do an array of things and not every human being can do everything well. Most of the time, it's about how much trust in ourselves that we can allow ourselves to learn how to do things that make us most uncomfortable.

May 20

Today's Games

"Yesterday's home runs don't win today's
games."
— Babe Ruth[106]

*W*e can't rely on yesterday's accomplishments to make things happen today. We
can look at yesterday's accomplishments as an
indicator that there is a greater possibility that
we may succeed. We still have to put in the hard
work and time for that to happen. We still have
to adjust our behaviors to the new obstacles that
we will face before we're successful. There will
be still a struggle, but hopefully, we've learned
something from our past accomplishments so
we can do better today. We gain confidence
when we've gotten through obstacles. That's
what is so satisfying getting to the other side
and looking at how far we've grown. We have to
learn continuously and improve our craft or, at
least, maintain it.

May 21

Still Moving Forward

"Even if you fall on your face, you're still moving forward." — Victor Kiam[107]

It gives us hope that as long as we get up from a fall, we're still moving forward. We're still chasing our dreams. We haven't given up. Our eyes are still on the goal. There will always be delays and setbacks during our journey, and that's all. We continue because the fall just makes us stronger than before when we get back up. It may seem like we're going at a snail pace and that's okay to take our time if we need to. We created regrets when we gave up because of our self-doubts. Yes, we all have a life to live and have responsibilities to keep, however, we don't have to stop pursuing our goals unless we have a desire to stop and make peace with it and move on.

May 22

It's What You See

"It's not what you look at that matters, it's what you see." — Henry David Thoreau[108]

$\mathcal{A}$ n empty mind sees little to no opportunities in his or her life. However, a creative mind looks for opportunities and see them and then use them. Sometimes we see no opportunity because our scope of the world is small. We begin to see opportunities when our world expanse. We begin to build new associations and see that we have more choices than we thought we didn't have before. We dropped the veils from our eyes, and we can see things clearer. These new associations are life-changing. We won't ever have to go back to what was. We have a new way of thinking about things and life. Our stress level is down because the weight of the world is much lighter. We're light as a feather because we let go of unnecessary worries and turn our attention to much broader things that are more meaningful in our lives than before.

May 23

Know Better, Then Do Better

"Do the best you can until you know better.
Then when you know better, do better."
— Maya Angelou[109]

$\mathcal{A}$s Maya Angelou says that we can only do our best from what we know. Learning a new thing is always a learning curve. We got to be patient with ourselves. It is also all right to ask someone for help if we need it. Sometimes our pride gets in the way when we need someone's help. Well, it is time to put our pride aside temporarily and ask for help as needed. We don't have the expertise for everything. When someone asks for our expertise about something we know, we're willing to give our opinion, and we feel good afterward about it. So, let us do the same, ask another. Once we get some recommendations, then we can make things better because we know better, and now we can do better.

May 24

The One Reason It Works

**"Forget all the reasons it won't work and be-
lieve the one reason that it will."
— Unknown[110]**

*W*e tell ourselves it won't work because
then we won't have to put in the time
and hard work. However, if it's something excit-
ing that it might work and we want it to work,
then we will find a way to make it work. We will
form a strategy and a plan to create an atmosphere of optimism. We need the confidence
to help us to be willing to look for novel solu-
tions and to be encouraged to think of different
ways so we won't be tethered down by biases.
We can find plenty of reasons not to move forward in our endeavors and passions. But why
should we deny our efforts and desires especially when those things defined who we are? It's
not too late to design our path.

May 25

Logic and Imagination

> "Logic will get you from A to B. Imagination
> will take you everywhere."
> — Albert Einstein[111]

*Y*es, logic can only do some much for us. Logic can restrict our imagination. A mind that imagines is like kids running around playing, touching, and seeing and experiencing their environment. When we use our imagination, we are expressing freely our mind. We're allowing ourselves to see things that we haven't seen before. Just as Albert Einstein says in the quote that imagination can take us everywhere we want to go. Imagination helps us to get the picture just right in our head. Imagination cultivates an initial idea in something we can touch or experience. After we'd exercised our minds through imagination, we then can use the critical part of our brain to make logic out of ideas we got from our imagination.

May 26

Let Go of Yesterday

"Why let go of yesterday? Because yesterday has already let go of you." — Steve Maraboli[112]

*W*e hold on to something like the past because it is familiar to us even though what we hang on to is unhealthy or self-destructive. Because it's familiar to us doesn't mean we have to hold on to it. Letting go of the past can be painful but necessary, and the pain is temporary. We may have some anxiety because we're afraid of being alone. We can always replace loneliness with a goal or a hobby. Yesterday is just a memory nothing more and nothing less. We just have the footprints of yesterday. Yesterday is just a shadow that's been skewed by our biases and background. Yesterday doesn't have to have power over our thoughts or affect how we live our lives today. We're able to live our lives today when we let go of yesterday.

May 27

Light Tomorrow

> "Light tomorrow with today!"
> — Elizabeth Barrett Browning[113]

$\mathcal{A}$ nother way we light up tomorrow is not going to bed angry at someone. Instead, we resolve it with the person or let go of it before we retire. We can light up tomorrow by not worrying about tomorrow. We can light up tomorrow if we trust more of ourselves today. We can light up tomorrow if we're connecting with good people today. No matter how unpleasant the weather looks tomorrow— whether there will be snowing or raining— tomorrow will be lit because of today. Since we have today to spend our time, we might as well be productive; so, when tomorrow comes, we will be better off than we were yesterday.

May 28

No Failures...Just Experiences

"There are no failures. Just experiences and your reactions to them." — Tom Krause[114]

*F*ailures are just our expectations not being met. When our standards are too high, it is inevitable we will fail to meet them. It is like a self-fulfilling prophecy. But, if we could lower our standards, then it would be possible to allow ourselves the room to make mistakes, to learn and make improvements from them. We don't have to be so hard on ourselves that we don't allow ourselves the luxury of failing while learning something new. We are not robots where every movement we make is with precision and every thought calculated. We are human beings that make our way through our experiences.

May 29

Important Work

"Your most important work is always ahead of you, never behind you." — Stephen Covey[115]

*Y*es, we can see that we're making progress by looking back at the work we have done. When we rise in the morning, we can be thankful that we have another day to do our important work. Our important work is ahead of us because we know our purpose. We know what's important to us, therefore, we want to continue doing the work. It's our labor of love because it bears meaning to us. A life without a purpose is no life at all. Our purpose gives us value in the work we do, and that's important to us. Our aim is what drives us to continue the work even though at times no one understands why we do it.

May 30

Managing and Anticipating

"Anticipate the difficult by managing the easy." — Lao Tzu[116]

$\mathcal{W}$e tend to place our attention on the difficult part of learning than managing the easy parts. Keeping our attention on the difficult parts will only discourage us from learning how to do things. Why not find out how to handle the easy parts first and worry about the difficult parts later. Learning the easy part is not to avoid learning the difficult, however, to get us more acquainted and familiar with our learning. Repetition will be useful once we begin to learn the difficult parts because it will get easier to do. It is always better to break down the hard parts into smaller ones because that way they will be a lot easier to manage.

May 31

What We Know We Can Be

"We cannot become what we need to be by remaining what we are." — Max de Pree[117]

*W*e can never stop growing. Don't we want to learn something about ourselves that we didn't know before? We're full of untapped potentials. These possibilities are waiting for us to be used to assist us in becoming what we need to be. We have the opportunities to do something new that we don't often do. We have to change the way we think. We're evolving every day which means we continue adjusting and adapting to our new way of doing and thinking. We're challenged by external forces as well as internal ones. No one is without a challenge in life. We all have to deal with different types of challenges all of our lives. However, each one of us deals with challenges in our unique way as we're becoming more of what we can be.

June 1

A Positive Attitude

"The only disability in life is a bad attitude."
— Scott Hamilton[118]

*I*f only the disability in life is a bad attitude, then the potential in life is a positive one. We can change our attitude from a negative to a positive one. We can better handle stressful situations if we have a positive attitude than if we have a negative one that can only exacerbate an already difficult situation. When we see things positively, we can think better and have more energy. A bad attitude can zap away the energy from our bodies that can lead our minds to more black and white thinking. In that state, we can't see alternatives. We need to see that we have alternatives so we can act precisely as a positive attitude can get us much farther ahead in life.

June 2

God Gave Us Friends

"Friends are the siblings God never gave us."
— Mencius[119]

*W*e all need a friend or two to hang out. We have friends that share common interests. We need friends that are honest with us, and we are with them. It is nice to look forward to seeing a friend we haven't seen for a long time. It is nice to reminisce with friends about the stupid things we did in our youth. A good friend challenges us to do our best despite our hesitation, and we reciprocate the challenge. A friend accepts our flaws but challenges us not to be hindered by them. Friendship can last a lifetime. However, we can lose a friend quicker than we think. Friendship is a bonding experience with another person or person(s). Let us never take our close friendships for granted because before you know it they're gone.

June 3

Creating Yourself

"Life isn't about finding yourself. Life is about creating yourself." — George Bernard Shaw[120]

*T*o find one's self implies that we are lost, and we don't know who we are or who we are supposed to be. However, to create one's self means that we know who we are and what we want in life. We base our decisions on what we want in life. We create a plan, and we follow that plan we have laid out for ourselves to help us to achieve our goals and desires. We learn a skill or a craft so we can become who we wish to be in our lives. For us to be something, we must practice and use every opportunity to use our skills in real life. We create ourselves by the choices we've made up to this point. It is not by coincidence where we are in our lives today. The decisions and choices we made in the past are the results of what we're doing today with our lives. The decisions and choices we made in the past created who and what we are today.

June 4

Luck Will Find You

"I've found that luck is quite predictable. If you want more luck, take more chances. Be more active. Show up more often."
— Brian Tracy[121]

In other words, luck is not handed to us. We have to work for luck for it to happen. We have to be where everything is going on for us to get some good luck. Luck is not created in a vacuum. We don't have to give up on luck when we've been at it for such a long time. We have a greater chance of luck when we continue to participate in the work we do that gives us passion. Passion is more important than luck because passion lasts longer than luck. Luck is being at the right place and at the right time and meeting the right person that can alter our course to the next level if the opportunity presents itself to show our talents. Luck is not idle. It looks for that person who is ready to be what they have always been.

June 5

Problems Are Guidelines

"Problems are not stop sign; they are
guidelines."
— Robert H. Schuller[122]

*P*roblems are inevitable. We will always have them in our lives. We just have to learn how to deal and sometimes adapt to our problems. We got to continue living because the world won't stop when we have a problem. We can see a problem as a guideline. They tell us about ourselves. Not every problem is going to be resolved right away. If we're still dealing with an old problem, then that tells us that we haven't learned how to handle the problem. We're still distorting reality instead of dealing with reality as is. We still have some growing up to do. The problem can be a reoccurring theme in our lives if we don't let go. However, we must. We need to let go and use what capabilities we do have to resolve and accept the problem and then move on.

June 6

The Curious Paradox

"The curious paradox is that when I accept myself just as I am, then I can change."
— Carl Rogers[123]

So most of us may think regarding what we don't accept or dislike about ourselves, we must change. However, Carl Roger was trying to explain to us that it is easier to make a change if we first accept the parts that we dislike about ourselves. Yes, we can accept all our foibles; however, it's hard to change every foible. We can change some things that are maybe affecting our relationships or job performance. Interestingly, we can hone in on someone else's liabilities better than we see our own. What we dislike the most in someone else's is surely a reflection of our self. Although it's hard to change ourselves, it is not impossible as long we're aware of what we need to be modified. Again, let us accept ourselves before we do anything to make a change because we owe that to ourselves and others.

June 7

Make Dreams, Then Make Realities

"We all have dreams. But in order to make dreams come into reality, it takes an awful lot of determination, dedication, self-discipline, and effort." — Jesse Owens[124]

Having a dream is nice. Dreams can make us hopeful amid a struggle. With determination, dedication, self-discipline, and effort we still need to keep our eyes on the ball. We still need to be reminded as to why we started. What motivated us to begin in the first place? There are times that we want to give up when things don't work out. We will make mistakes, but we can learn from them. We can take breaks in between our efforts. We can also reward ourselves each time we reach a milestone. We won't know what we're doing at first, but each day we get better and thus become more efficient in our work. We're competing with ourselves, not with someone else. It is our dream we're fulfilling, not someone else's. It is our treasure chest of experiences from our determination, dedication, that we will find what's meaningful and most fulfilling.

June 8

Be True to Yourself

"Above all, be true to yourself, and if you cannot put your heart in it, take yourself out of it."— Unknown[125]

If we offer to pay someone for services, we expect to have top-notch services. No one wants to hire someone to do a half-hearted job. Just the same for us, if we aren't into what we do and our hearts aren't into it, we owe it to ourselves, to take ourselves out of it. Instead, we find something else to do that we find satisfying and make us happy. It is really about how true to ourselves we are. We don't have to do this or that thing to satisfy another person or because society says we're supposed to do this or that thing. If we're authentic and feel comfortable in our own skin, then like-minded people will come around us because of us. Real people attract other real people.

June 9

Believe It

"To accomplish great things, we must not only act, but also dream; not only plan, but also believe." — Anatole France[126]

*W*hen we dream about it, we see our future selves doing great things. Dreaming is the beginning of our journey. We want to make our lives better and the lives of others. Our actions make things happen, and our dreams are the fuel that keeps us moving toward that goal. But before we act, we create a plan to follow so we don't get off track and modify it as we need to. When we believe it, we see ourselves carrying out the plan. Sure, there are some doubts, however, without a plan, there will be more doubts to deal with. As we follow the plan, we see that our doubts diminish over time. Dreaming it into reality is not an easy task, but it is doable.

June 10

Create a Life Worth Living

"Believe that life is worth living and your
belief will help create the fact."
— William James[127]

I f we believe that life is worth living, then
we look for things that will help us live a
worthy life. We will create a life worth living
because we have self-worth. Somebody believes
in us, and therefore, we believe in ourselves. We
have something to contribute that makes us
worthy as no one is better than another. It is
hard for someone to have self-worth when they
have lost everything, like their family, friends,
house, etc. For us to still have these things, we
can help those who have fallen if they want it.
We can only guide and be a light to help them
along the way to their path. Once upon a time,
we needed help and was thankful that someone
cared whether it was emotionally or physically.

June 11

A Flexible Approach

"Stay committed in your decisions, but stay flexible in your approach." — Tom Robbins[128]

*F*lexibility is the high mark for growth and understanding. Flexibility requires us to have an open mind to new things. Learning and flexibility can go hand and hand. Everyone has biases. They keep our mind closed which keep us from learning and experiencing new things. When we keep our approach flexible as Tom Robbins suggested, we are trying different kinds of approaches until we find what works and what doesn't work. Change requires us to be flexible, so we don't injure ourselves physically or psychologically. If we want to stimulate some excitement in our lives, we must learn to be more flexible. We can be flexible but also cautious at the same time. Having the right balance will do.

June 12

Compasses Toward Growth

"Fear, uncertainty, and discomfort are your
compasses toward growth."
— Celestine Chua[129]

We can use fear to motivate us or allow our
fear to control us. We can use fears as our
compass to help us test the water before swimming. Fear can help us to determine whether or
not if it is safe to move forward. We can take
small chances to keep our fear in check. We will
never be one hundred percent certain about anything. Uncertainties are a part of life. We can feel
uncertain and still move forward anyway. As we
move forward, we will begin to uncover or erase
some uncertainties we have in our minds that
are unreal and untrue. When we're presenting
with something that we feel out of control, we
experience discomfort. We can learn to be comfortable in an uncomfortable situation. Taking
risks will always be a part of life.

June 13

Inspiration from Hard Hits and Problems

"Life becomes inspiring, not in spite of the
problems and the hard hits, but because of
them."
— Joni Eareckson Tada[130]

*W*e can all relate to problems and hard hits
in our lives. We learn to get through
problems as long as we live. Problems and hard
hits are part of life and nature's way of us learning how to manage through life without our
problems getting us down. We can see inspiration when we see someone pull themselves out
of a deep hole or someone triumph over adversity. We can learn that if someone can triumph
against all odds, we can also find that strength
within ourselves to push ourselves harder up
the mountain. The examples of the triumph of
others can evoke in us the motivation to strive to
be our best selves amid problems.

June 14

Success and Failure

"Never let success go to your head and never
let failure go to your heart."
— Ziad K. Abdelnour[131]

*I*t takes maturity to learn from our failures. Failure can give us a free education. Failure can prove more valuable to us than success. It tells us what actions to take and what actions to discontinue. Failure can tell us how much we need to improve before we succeed. Therefore, failure should go to our heads so we can analyze the pattern and alter our behavior accordingly. Success is difficult. Success can never be maintained for very long. There are peaks and valleys. Failures and successes are part of the game of life. We can learn about life from both failures and successes. No one is exempt from failure. We need both our hearts and our heads to work together regarding success and failure. They say we should follow our hearts; we need our heads to keep us in check.

June 15

Character, Commitment and Discipline

"It was character that got us out of bed, commitment that moved us into action, and discipline that enabled us to follow through."
— Zig Ziglar[132]

*C*haracter, commitment, and discipline are elements of a successful life. Most of us know this to be true. However, it is important to be reminded. When we had a hard day, we can say to ourselves that we're building character. When we get frustrated with something, we can say to ourselves to stay disciplined and keep ourselves together. When we struggle to get something done, we can say to ourselves that we're committed to the task because it is important to us and that we will follow through with what we've started. If we want something, it will require all three of these elements. There is no such thing as a free lunch. We're happier when we earn our keep. We feel good about ourselves because we did something for ourselves.

June 16

Doing, Being and Becoming

"Life's not about expecting, hoping and wishing, it's about doing, being and becoming."
— Mike Dooley[133]

*W*ishing for something tells us we have a desire. Hoping for something tells us we're looking into the future for something good to happen. Expecting says we want something to happen sooner than in the future. However, if we do more doing, we're expressing what we want to become. What we do come out of what we are. Being is our natural state, and it takes less energy to do. Becoming will take us a lifetime to develop who we are and what we want to be is what we're wishing, expecting, and hoping for in our lives today. Life is about experiencing, sharing, and living. How do we learn from life if we're not expressing our uniqueness to ourselves and the world? We are here to be.

June 17

Prepare to Succeed

"By failing to prepare, you are preparing to fail." — Benjamin Franklin[134]

*I*f we fail to prepare, we presuppose failure. Therefore, we fail. However, if we prepare ourselves to do the work that's required of us, then we presuppose success. Therefore, we succeed. By what we do, our actions are demonstrating to ourselves that we will succeed. We learn better by doing the action. The results of our actions will always be our proof that we're succeeding. Just as the results of our inactions will always be our proof that we're not succeeding, thus substantiate our belief to fail. We just have to discern which behaviors we are using to get us closer to our goals and which ones are not. We can easily distract ourselves from what we supposed to be doing to prepare ourselves for success. And it takes just as much energy doing nothing as it is doing something so we might as well use the energy productively.

June 18

Starting with a Small Seed

"From a small seed a mighty trunk may grow."
— Aeschylus[135]

The easiest way to build confidence is if we set obtainable goals that we know we can do. Each time we accomplish a goal our self-reliance increases and we begin to feel comfortable doing it. It doesn't mean it will be easy completing the goal, but it does mean that we have more confidence that we will reach our goal. It is important to stay consistent, and laser-focused so there won't be room for distractions until our goal is completed. It is a good idea to establish a routine to help keep us consistent.

June 19

Be As You Wish

"Be as you wish to seem." — Socrates[136]

*W*e don't have to seem to be a certain way. Instead, we can be a certain way. We don't have to project to others what we wish to appear, however, be what we want to seem. In other words, be ourselves. We like what we're becoming. We do things we enjoy doing. We're defined by what we do. What we are is what we do. The decisions we make in our life are based on who we are today. However, we change over time, and we readjust with changes that come our way. It's all right to embrace what we wish to seem to others so we can be fully ourselves. It is much easier being ourselves than being something we're not. It takes less energy just to be.

June 20

Delay or Conquer

"What you deny or ignore, you delay. What
you accept and face, you conquer."
— Robert Tew[137]

*W*hen we deny or ignore something, it all
comes from our fears. We're afraid to
know the truth and reality of things. We prefer
to hold on to a distorted reality that we've created. And we think that's going to keep us safe.
Worrying about things can't save us. Worrying
has no power. However, if we face things as they
are, then we have one another to face things together. Denial is another word for distraction.
We deliberately distract ourselves because we
don't want to face what might cause us pain. So
how can we conquer something unknown to us
without investigating? Knowledge is powerful.
Knowledge can subside our fears if we allow
ourselves to be open to it.

June 21

Remaking Life after Grief

"Grief is in two parts. The first is loss. The second is the remaking of life." — Anne Roiphe[138]

*W*e all have experienced grief when we lose someone close to our hearts. It can be difficult sometimes for us to move on since it feels like a part of us has also died. However, we still have the other part of us that can keep the lost individual alive in our hearts. If we retain the memory of the lost loved one alive, then they will be with us for the rest of our lives. When we recall a pleasant memory of a person who passed away, our brain won't know the difference. We will still experience a good feeling and even some comfort. The most difficult thing to do is to let go and move on as life continues.

June 22

Stimulating Learning

"Be thankful when you don't know something for it gives you the opportunity to learn."
— Unknown[139]

Sometimes we get quickly caught up in thinking we don't know enough about things. We don't have to feel that we're behind in our understanding of things. No one person knows everything. It is better to have more than one mind working together because together, we can solve problems better and faster. It is better to learn from someone who has knowledge and experience on a subject. Sometimes we feel inadequate about our lack of knowledge as our egos get in the way. Each time that happens it is just another opportunity to learn something new that will hopefully stimulate our imagination into coming up with new ideas.

June 23

Facing Reality

"Not everything that is faced can be changed, but nothing can be changed until it is faced." — James Baldwin[140]

If we start to face reality as it is, then we begin to truly live our lives. We truly live our lives is when we learn to rely more on ourselves. We rediscover we can do things. There were times in our past that we had to face things we didn't think we could get through, and we did. No matter how much we are in denial about stuff, we can never fool ourselves. There are some things we have to admit to ourselves. Facing reality is not always an easy thing to do. But we face things anyways because facing things allow us to make a shift in our lives and grow into our selves.

June 24

What We Cling To

> "You only lose what you cling to."
> — Buddha[141]

The above quote reminds me of a paradox or oxymoron. Buddha is saying if we just stop desiring something that we don't have, then we will lose out on what we already possess inside of us. Sometimes we think we need to have something more because someone possesses it. We may have noticed that our desire is the greatest when someone has something we want. However, if we let those things go, then we would have everything. We just have to look into ourselves and discover what we have and bring it to the surface. When we discover what we possess within, we no longer have to make a comparison. We no longer have a desire to look outside ourselves to fulfill a void that we have created.

June 25

Commitment, Conflict and Character

"Commitment in the face of conflict produces character." — Unknown[142]

*I*f we want to meet our goals, then we must commit to the things we need to do to complete them. Commitment means doing something for the long haul despite the difficulties, or the time constraints we will face. Dedication and determination go hand and hand. We may have doubts about our abilities to complete our goals, or we don't feel like doing it. However, we continue to strive to do it anyhow because we know it could make us grow. Growth can build character if we're willing to put up with delays, obstacles, and frustrations to get there.

June 26

When We're Proud

"I still have a long way to go, but I'm already so far from where I used to be, and I'm proud of that." — Unknown[143]

*W*hatever efforts we've been putting into such as our projects and our goals, we should be proud of ourselves. Sometimes we wish that things would move along quickly because we want to see the result. In the beginning, we have to be a little patient when we're at the beginning stages while our brains are becoming acquainted with everything. It takes time for the new things we're learning to stick. We know this from life experience that later in our learnings when everything begins to click. We then look back and wonder why we didn't understand things sooner. We must allow time to show us when we're ready to accept some new understanding.

June 27

Today's Shade

"Someone is sitting in the shade today because someone planted a tree a long time ago."
— **Warren Buffett**[144]

*E*very day we see the fingerprints and footprints of our ancestors. Some of us live in homes that were built in the 1920s, and there are people today in other countries live in castles, sanctuaries, houses that were build centuries ago. Some of our infrastructures are based on Roman architecture. We like to create things to make things easier for ourselves and the next generation.

We passed down our values to the younger generation so they won't make the same mistake as we once did. We have advanced technology because of what started at the beginning. It's what others strived to do that they laid a foundation so we can solve today's problems more sufficiently. We may wonder if this knowledge is somehow passed down through our DNA or civilization has created an atmosphere that each generation has an opportunity to better his or her life.

185

June 28

Lessons, Acceptance and Gratitude

"No regrets, just lessons. No worries, just acceptance. No expectations, just gratitude. Life is too short." — Unknown[145]

*I*f we turn our regrets into lessons, we will learn something of value. If we lessen our worries, then we would live our lives better. If we lower our expectations, then we would be happier. Our regrets can keep us in the past while our worries keep us fearing the future. Our expectations can keep us disappointed in life. Lessons we learn from life will keep things interesting while acceptance will keep us in peace. Our gratitude will keep us focusing on the things that matter the most.

June 29

Similar Values in Friendship

"The person who doesn't value you is blocking you from the one who will. Let them go." — Robert Tew[146]

*W*e're wasting our time trying to get the approval of a person who doesn't care about what we do. We ought to care about what we do. The person we need to impress and please the most is ourselves. That's how we build our confidence in ourselves is by doing the things that please us. We're content when we please ourselves because we don't have to seek outside ourselves for the satisfaction that we can get from it for ourselves. Friendship is built on having similar values. A friend allows us to be ourselves while we're not afraid to allow our friends to be themselves around us.

June 30

How Do We React?

> "Stress and unhappiness come not from situations, but how you respond to situations." — Brian Tracy[147]

It's hard for us to make the distinction between an event and our reaction to an event or a situation. There are facts, and there are opinions about the facts. We all come from different backgrounds where we see events through. Some of us are more affected by an event than others. It depends on how we're raised and what are our values. We see things through our values. It's all right to leave an unpleasant event if it's affecting us. No one has the right to force us to stay at a place that's unpleasant to us. As adults, we are responsible for ourselves. Lowering our expectations is an excellent way to reduce our stress level and to better handle ourselves in awkward situations.

July 1

A Time for Sorrow and a Time for Joy

> "Today's a good day to start walking in the opposite direction of anything or anyone that causes you more sorrow than joy."
> — Mandy Hale[148]

*S*ome sorrow is a given. It is part of life to experience. However, joy is also a part of life to experience. If we experience pain most of our days, then it is time to walk in the opposite direction because it is too difficult to find joy in sorrow. We do need to experience all our emotions in life. That's what makes life colorful and meaningful instead of us looking at the world in black and white where there are no feelings and no emotions. There is a time for sorrow, and there is time for joy in our lives.

July 2

Tomorrow Is Ours to Win or Lose

"Yesterday is not ours to recover, but tomorrow is ours to win or lose." — Lyndon B. Johnson[149]

*W*e no longer can touch yesterday. Yesterday is just a slight or skewed distortion of our memory. We can't always trust our minds implicitly because we tend to fill in the gaps to complete a memory. Memories are like many pieces to a puzzle that has scattered; we have to find them to put back together again. It is not always easy to do. When tomorrow becomes today, we have another opportunity to get back in the battle of life to win some and to lose some. We won't always be winners, and we won't always be losers, but we can participate in life to learn our way around.

July 3

The Point of All Achievement

"The starting point of all achievement is desire." — Napoleon Hill[150]

If we have the desire to start something, then let us do it. We satisfy a desire by doing it. And we will be most satisfied when we achieve what we set out to do. Our passion for work will get us through the difficult times. We just continue listening to our hearts because our hearts will lead us where we wish. Our minds will make sure that the heart is staying on track. If we want something, it won't be easy to get, but it is possible if we possess the laser-sharp focus because that's when will get many things accomplished.

July 4

Enjoying Life through Independence

"Don't wait for everything to be perfect before
you decide to enjoy your life."
— Joyce Meyer[151]

*W*e need to stop waiting on the perfect set-up before we can enjoy life. Preparation is one thing, but stalling for perfection is another. The only way we can enjoy life is if we experience things as is. Accepting things that we don't have control over is the first step. We do have control, for the most part, ourselves. Perfection is in the mind of the beholder. What seems perfect for one person may not be perfect for another. Perfection is just a fantasy world made up of our need for protection from hurts and disappointments. Enjoying our lives is how we express our independence and freedoms, not through perfectionism.

July 5

Impossible Until It's Done

"It always seems impossible until it's done."
— Nelson Mandela[152]

*W*henever we see another person do an extraordinary thing, we think it's no way we can do something extraordinary like that. We forget that we've already done things we thought were impossible to do. When trying something new, we thought it was impossible to do but somehow after putting in a lot of effort, we kept at it. We stayed with it long enough that we began to see the progress that our confidence started to grow as the hard work began to pay off. So, what was extraordinary is that we started to believe in ourselves.

July 6

The Human Spirit

*W*e need each other more than ever when disaster strikes. When we work together and have a common cause anything is possible. The human spirit always transcends adversities. We somehow get through difficulties when it seems impossible at the moment to move forward. Action is one of the most powerful agents we can use to get through things. When life-changing events affect us directly or indirectly as a people, we need to come together and help one another to get through them. We don't have to feel alone in a time of need. We can always uplift one another when we're down.

July 7

Chance to be Better

"Freedom is nothing but a chance to be better."
— Albert Camus[154]

*N*o one wants to be or feel restricted. Interestingly, that Albert Camus linked 'freedom' and 'chance to be better,' together. If we think about it, we do need room to improve ourselves. Freedom means going beyond our tethers. We don't want to be locked into one place. We want to spread our wings so we can fly. Freedom creates a spacious environment, so we have a better chance of growth. Freedom is the foundation of responsibility. We are free to respond to the needs of others and ourselves. We become better people when we're released from our tethers. If we don't know we're freed, then how can we know we have a chance to be better.

July 8

Work Has Its Own Reward

"Work is not man's punishment. It is his reward and his strength and his pleasure."
— George Sand[155]

*W*ork gives us a healthy dose of self-confidence each day. Work brings us out of ourselves. Although we may complain sometimes, we still get our pleasure out of work. We grow in strength when we have pulled through a stressful workday. We can stand proud of ourselves. We like it when we get things done. At times our job is overwhelming us with a lot to do in a short amount of time, but somehow, we get things done, and we're happy and relieved. All in all, no one can take away our experiences. The best reward is that we can take them with us wherever we go.

July 9

Going Back to Our Roots

Going back to our roots doesn't necessarily mean digging up our genealogy. It could mean just looking back to our earlier learnings. For example, we can reminisce about the music we once grew up with. Music can easily bring us back to that time of our lives when things were simple and innocent. It can take us back to a time where we didn't have a care in the world because it was our parents' job to worry about things. We were urged to be children and play outside and be adventuresome and learn about our surroundings that we didn't understand. As children our world was new and we experienced everything thoroughly. If only we experience a little of that as an adult, we would be less cynical about our world.

July 10

Attitude Makes a Difference

> "Make your optimism come true."
> — Unknown[156]

It is better to have an optimistic attitude than to have a pessimistic one. It is our attitude that affects our world and how we live our lives. We have ups and downs in our lives. It is how we live our lives despite the ups and downs (especially the downs) that we all have in our life. Besides our downs are temporary, and only part of our life, and we can make a choice not to be defended by them. We can see them as the roughages of life that each one of us experiences. We can make optimism real in our lives by creating an atmosphere of living our lives to the fullest.

July 11

A Listening Ear

"Sometimes, what a person needs is not a brilliant mind that speaks, but a patient heart that listens." — Unknown[157]

*W*e don't have to win an argument or have the last word to feel good about ourselves. We don't even have to always be right about something. There will come a time when we will be right, but even then, we can be silent. We can be great listeners, because it's alright that the other person has an opportunity to be heard. Hearing someone vent can be painful to our ears, but if we do, that person will remember us as a good listener. And, being a good listener bridges a deep connection. We come to the conversation with different perspectives, but instead of convincing the other person that we're right, why not just listen? Although there are some who will dominate the conversation after some time listening, we can politely thank the other person for sharing and that it is time to go to a preplanned engagement or to return to work.

July 12

A Different Light

"Always end the day with a positive thought. No matter how hard things were, tomorrow's a fresh opportunity to make it better."
— Unknown[158]

*W*hen we had a bad day, it is easier to spend time obsessing over the unpleasant events. Spending time obsessing over them only makes it difficult to end the day with positive thoughts. Having a bad day doesn't mean that our whole day was bad. Because it started badly doesn't mean we have to end our day badly. Discounting the positive is counterproductive. We can always find something positive in our day. That's where having a sense of humor can come into play, because humor can help us look at a difficult situation in a different light.

July 13

Dancing in the Rain of Life

"Life isn't about waiting for the storm to pass. It's about learning how to dance in the rain." — Vivian Greene[159]

*L*ife is never going to be exactly the way we think it should be. We have no control over that. But for us to reduce our anxiety we ought to learn to accept the roughages of life because this is how we embrace life and how we feel most alive. This is how we dance in the rain of life. Since we're a part of life, let us participate instead of standing on the sideline of life. We're going to get some bumps and bruises, but we will also get some life back into our lives.

July 14

A Different Angle

> "Vitality shows in not only the ability to per-
> sist but the ability to start over."
> — F. Scott Fitzgerald[160]

Starting over doesn't mean it is the end of the world. It doesn't mean we've wasted time. It is better to start something over sooner rather than later. It becomes a problem when we're doing the same things repeatedly while expecting a better outcome. It is better to try different approaches or look at the problem from a different angle. We can be persistent all we want to, but if we continue without reconsidering another way, then we're doomed to cliché patterns that only gets us nowhere. Instead, we have an opportunity to start over with a different way of looking at things.

July 15

New Choices Today

> "Every day brings new choices."
> — Martha Beck[161]

$\mathcal{E}$ very day is an opportunity to make a choice or accurately make new choices. Choices are as full as our minds. It depends on the mind, how many options we can see that are in front of us. It is not enough to see the choices; we can select some that are relevant to our situation. Some decisions are life-changing that can affect our entire life. Behind the choices we make, comes an opportunity to shake up our world. Every day also brings us an opportunity to make our lives better than before if we want. If we're already content with our lives, then we can be grateful that we have another day to express our essential self.

July 16

Imagine It, Achieve It, and Become It

> "If you can imagine it, you can achieve it. If you can dream it, you can become it."
> — William Arthur Ward[162]

*I*ncredibly, we can imagine an idea and turn it into something real that can affect everyone who touches it or are touched by it. It is wonderful that we can dream of doing something in our future self that keeps us going today. The power of our imagination is that we can see it in our mind's eyes the way we want it before it's ever created. In our dreams we see ourselves doing what we most want or desire in our lives and become it if we want it bad enough.

July 17

No Two Are Alike

"Every building is a prototype. No two are alike."— Helmut Jahn[163]

*W*e're just like a building, no two are alike. We're born original. So, our goal in life is to be original and stay unique which means to grow into ourselves. We should be what we're intended to be because we will be happier in the long run. We will be able to express honestly to the world what we always meant to be because we can be true to ourselves and others. We can all bring our unique styles together, and that's what makes the world interesting with a lot of variety. Variety is more stimulating to our senses. We don't need to copy someone else's uniqueness but we can become more of our own unique selves.

July 18

Breathe, Step Back, Think

> "Breathe. Step back. Think. Then react. "
> — Unknown[164]

Sometimes our mouth moves before we think. Sometimes we see the trees before we step back to see the forest. Sometimes we forget to breathe before we react. When breathing normally, we're getting more oxygen to our brain. Then maybe we're getting the opportunity to think clearly about seeing the event at a wider scope. When we put events into a different perspective, we have the chance to react appropriately with clarity and not so much with a knee jerk.

July 19

Heart of Hearts

"We cannot achieve more in life than what we
believe in our heart of hearts we deserve to
have."— James R. Ball[165]

If we find ourselves not achieving what
we set out to do, then maybe it's because
we don't believe in our hearts that we deserve
success, or because we don't believe in ourselves. We only deserve success when we know
in our hearts that we've worked so hard to
achieve it. We got to believe in ourselves even
for the possibility of success. It's all right to have
ambitions in life to help motivate us. We have as
much right to have deserved success just as
anyone else.

July 20

Out of Difficulties

"Out of difficulties grow miracles."
— Jean de la Gruyere[166]

*O*ut of difficulties, we learn something about ourselves that we haven't known before. We've discovered how strong we've become. We've learned that we can rely on ourselves more and make things happen with our actions. Life difficulties can reveal to us our true character to ourselves and others. When we see a challenging and daunting task in front of us to do, our body has the urge to resist. However, if we proceed with the task, we have conquered ourselves, and that's extraordinary, thus a miracle. We have broken up the belief that we can't do something difficult through focus.

July 21

Find Yourself in the Present

"In the process of letting go you will lose many things from the past, but you will find yourself." — Deepak Chopra[167]

*I*n other words, we're not defined by our past. Therefore, we don't have to identify with the past as though that's all we live for. Our past is a reflection of what we did and experienced in our lives. Letting go means leaving the past behind us instead of looking into the lens of our past. We can look at what's in front, and we can plan for our future just as we planned long ago. What we do today is the result of what we did yesterday. We find ourselves in the present because we are not looking anywhere but in our present, where we can be at our best.

July 22

Generosity, Kindness, and Compassion

"Never define yourself by your relationship status, your income, or your looks. It's your generosity, kindness, and compassion that counts."— Brigitte Nicole[168]

*D*onating money is a generous offer, but money can only last so long. However, if we give our time to someone, then that may have an effect on that person for a lifetime. Compassion can heal a wounded soul in need and even the soul of the giver. We give without expecting anything in return because giving satisfies the conscience. Good looks are not everlasting. We can't stay young forever, but we can always strive to share our kindness.

July 23

A Clear Mind

"Keep your head clear. It doesn't matter how bright the path is if your head is always cloudy." — Unknown[169]

We even need our head clear when our path sometimes seems foggy, so we're able to maneuver better. For us to keep our minds clear, we need to make explicit what plan to execute. We need to write things down, so we have a better grip on them. And we need to re-mind ourselves what is our purpose when we first started on our path. Before we start any-thing, we can sit in a quiet place and allow our minds to clear up so we can be most effective.

July 24

Testing What's Possible

"You can do what's reasonable or you can decide what's possible." — Unknown[170]

$\mathcal{W}$ e can test what's possible in a reasonable way. We won't know if we don't test what's possible. We have to push the envelope to test to see what works and to understand why certain things won't work. This is a period when we gather information. This will help us open our minds for possibilities that we never thought about before. If we find ourselves not growing or not getting results, then we have to decide and test what's possible for ourselves.

July 25

Courage That Counts

"Success is never final, failure is never fatal. It's courage that counts." — John Wooden[171]

Success is telling us that whatever we're doing, we should continue to do it if we want it. If we see failures of ourselves and others as educational, then it's okay. It takes courage for us to fail and succeed. We need to experience both failure and success for us to deal with them. Courage helps us to take the necessary steps to get through the aftermath of success and failure. We must learn something about our struggles so that we can know ourselves better.

July 26

The Future Is Tomorrow

> "The best thing about the future is that it
> comes only one day at a time."
> — Dean Acheson[172]

So it is better to work on things today because we will know how much we've accomplished the next day. The day we start is the
day we begin to alter our future. We just have to
take action. The more we take action the closer
we get in meeting our future goals. So why do
we stall when we don't need to? A part of us
wants a change in our life, and another part of
us wants to stay in our comfort zone. Sometimes, there is an external conflict in what we
want to do. We're never going to be perfect if
we're waiting to plan out everything before we
start something. The sooner we start, the better
we are in the long run.

July 27

Digging Deeper

Sometimes we need to dig a little deeper to learn about ourselves. It is easier to stay on the surface of things than to dig deeper. Digging deeper is about stopping for a moment and paying closer attention to our behaviors, our thinking, and our feelings. It is easier to be on autopilot and not dig. But if we continue on autopilot, we continue to stay unchanged in our ways without an understanding of self. It is about knowing "thyself". It is learning about why we feel a certain way in one situation and don't feel a certain way in another. Learning about the self is a humbling and wonderful experience.

July 28

When the Mind Gains Strength

"In solitude the mind gains strength and learns to lean upon itself." — Laurence Sterne[173]

*E*very once in a while, we need some time to be alone so we can renew our strength. A time of solitude is a time to gather our thoughts and reflect on our life that we've lived so far. Solitude is a place where we may need some tuning up again. It is all right to revisit this place of solitude when we need to clear our heads so we can be at a level of strength to deal with everyday life again. We don't live in a vacuum, and we will be affected by life's challenges and worries. Therefore, some time away is necessary for us all.

July 29

Life Must Be Lived Forward

"Life can only be understood backwards; but it must be lived forwards."
— Soren Kierkegaard[174]

*I*n hindsight, life can be understood. It's hard to know our path, but we must continue forward. As long as we move along, we are creating a path for ourselves. Sitting idle while thinking about the past accomplishes nothing. As we move forward, we will make mistakes along the way, but it is a learning experience. Real knowledge is learning from our experiences, according to Albert Einstein.

July 30

Thought over Another

"The greatest weapon against stress is our ability to choose one thought over another." — William James[175]

A single thought can cause us stress in the body. And a single thought can cause us to experience relaxation. It all depends on which thoughts to pay attention to. If we have stress in our lives, then it is time to think about relaxation thoughts. We have to retrain ourselves to evoke relaxation thoughts when we're in a stressful situation. It takes practice each day to consciously think of positive thoughts for a certain period until we feel our bodies relaxing. We feel the tension leaves our body and when that happens, we can do a better job managing our stress.

July 31

Mental Attitude

"Happiness doesn't depend on any external conditions: it is governed by our mental attitude." — Dale Carnegie[176]

*I*f our mental attitude governs our happiness, then we have a choice and an opportunity to change our attitude. We don't have to be controlled by external forces or feel like they are controlling us. We can change our way of looking at external conditions that we think influences our attitude. We can always find something positive in an unpleasant event. When we find something positive in an unpleasant event, our mental attitude becomes hopeful.

August 1

Life Is Something We Do

"Life is something to do when you can't get to sleep." — Fran Lebowitz[177]

*T*hose are bonus hours, not insomnia hours; Milton Erickson once said to an insomniac. Instead of tossing and turning in bed for hours, we might as well use those hours to get something done. We sleep when we get sleepy. We do something while we're wide awake. Racing thoughts dissipate when we do something other than thinking about our thoughts. We place our attention on something externally which removes us from an endless internal dialogue about when we will fall asleep. After we do something satisfying, we start to get peace of mind and it is easier to fall fast asleep when we have a calming mind.

August 2

An Unfamiliar Path

"Don't be afraid to take an unfamiliar path. Sometimes they're the ones that take you to the best places." — Unknown[178]

*A*n unfamiliar path can easily evoke trepidation. However, once we get used to the path, our anxiety ceases. It is when we're standing next to the unfamiliar and not moving can provoke anxiety because we're anticipating danger. We don't know what is on the other side. That's why we must prepare ourselves as much as possible so we can be ready for the unexpected. Being ready for the unexpected changes our frame of mind because we're equipped to handle better whatever comes up.

August 3

Approving Yourself

"You have been criticizing yourself for years, and it hasn't worked. Try approving of yourself and see what happens."— Louise L. Hay[179]

If we're criticizing ourselves, then has it worked for us? If we're criticizing others, then have we asked ourselves has that person or persons made improvements? But, if we look back at our lives, we then see that criticism doesn't work. But if we shift our attention on accepting and approving of ourselves and others, then we permit ourselves to make a change for ourselves and not for someone else. We become models for others by our actions in how we conduct ourselves in the world. Self-accepting embraces and nurtures the mind, body, and soul.

August 4

Vision in Sight

"The only thing worse than being blind is having sight but no vision." — Helen Keller[180]

A vision is linked with having a purpose in our life. A vision is a glimpse into the future of how we want our life to be. We have to start now to make changes that will alter into something different in our future. Since tomorrow starts with our future, we're better off starting today because when tomorrow comes, we begin to see how things are changing in our lives. It starts with us to let our minds open so we clearly can see our vision we set before us. Today we plant seeds, water the soil, for a time, before we see satisfying results.

August 5

A Balance of Happiness and Sadness

*"The word 'happiness' would lose its meaning
if it were not balanced by sadness."*
— Carl Jung[181]

*W*e need to express both happiness and sadness. These emotions help us express how we feel at that moment in time. We have a range of emotions that we express daily. We ought not to be in a state of one emotion all the time. We need to allow ourselves to express all emotions. The feeling and expressing our emotions is natural. We get into trouble when we don't feel our feelings when it is necessary especially expressing the negative ones. Feeling is a product of what thoughts we are saying to ourselves and what constitutes sadness and happiness to us. What is important to us is where we feel very strongly towards it.

August 6

Welcome Change As the Rule

"You must welcome change as the rule but not
your ruler." — Denis Waitley[182]

*I*n other words, allow change to be an opportunity for growth and not allow
change to dominate our lives. Change is inevitable. We just have to respect and accept
change as it occurs without trying to fight it.
When we're at a certain level or if we go through
life's transitions we have to adapt to new
changes. Change disrupts our comfort zones.

For example, a spider has to find a se-
cluded area where a flying insect will happen to
go. After a spider spins its web and it is set up,
then the spider has to wait patiently for a catch.
Sometimes the web is never damaged or swept
away by a broom in a spider's lifetime and other
times a spider isn't so lucky when its web is
constantly destroyed.   But if the web is destroyed the spider will have to spin another web
because its life depends on it. We have to adapt
to change not be ruled by it.

August 7

Set a Peace of Mind

"Set peace of mind as your highest goal, and organize your life around it." — Brian Tracy[183]

*W*e all want peace in our lives. Sometimes we need to withdraw from our busy lives and to sit back and relax. When we slow down, our minds will slow down as well. It is nice to unwind. It is good for us to do so from time to time. We need to retreat when we're a little off-centered. It is a time to center ourselves so we can be at our best when we do return to the fast pace world. We can come back happier and recharged to take on the days. We return with a clear mind and we can see now our path or decisions we have that can make a difference in life.

August 8

Beyond What's Possible

"The limits of the possible can only be defined by going beyond them into the impossible."
— Arthur C. Clarke[184]

*I*t makes us wonder when we see what's possible. After we see what's possible, it makes one wonder what's beyond the possibility. But first, we must entertain the fact that what's possible and then have the courage to leap into the unknown that seems to be the impossible. What appears to be impossible is only a measure of what we don't know yet. We have to learn, experience, and be open to new ideas for us to get a glimpse of what is beyond the possible and into the impossible.

August 9

Made up of Small Deeds

"Great acts are made up of small deeds."
— Lao Tzu[185]

*W*e always want to get involved with the best part of a project. However, there will be times that we will have to do mundane parts of the project. There is usually the mundane or the small deeds that will help complete everything. We ought not to underestimate the little things we have to do because this stuff is the foundation of everything we do. Besides, it is much easier to manage the little things. Completing small tasks are always good reinforcer to encourage us to do more.

August 10

Find Your Purpose

"Your purpose in life is to find your purpose and give your whole heart and soul to it."
— Gautama Buddha[186]

*I*f we haven't given our whole heart and soul to something, then we haven't found our purpose. Besides, it's never too late to find our purpose as long as we're alive. If we want our remaining days or years to be meaningful, then we ought to make it our purpose to find what is our heart's desire in life. Our soul is waiting for us to make the move if we haven't done so already. Everyone is different when it comes to finding a purpose. One person may want to assist the homeless while another may want to save the environment. We all have unique talents like no other that can bring out our purpose in life. We shouldn't waste our talents when we can use them for the benefit of ourselves and others.

August 11

A Good Plan

> "A good plan today is better than a perfect plan tomorrow." — Proverb[187]

*W*hatever we plan doesn't have to be a perfect plan. When we plan today, we're oriented ourselves to the future. What we plan today helps us to fulfill our dreams for tomorrow. Planning today helps us to have more control over our future tomorrow. So, what we're doing today is what we planned yesterday. Today we have an opportunity to alter that plan. A plan to do something we've wanted to do for a while. There is no direction without a plan in our hands. Planning is an intellectual and a proactive exercise, not a reactionary one. We're forced to be concrete in our planning because we can see specifically what things we need to do to complete our goals.

August 12

Water the Grass Where We Stand

> "The grass is always greener where you water it." — Unknown[188]

*W*herever we go or whenever we leave for new endeavors, we have to make sure that the conditions are right before we do. Sometimes we want to do something else because we have this expectation that things will be better. Things will get better when we change not necessarily things around us change. If our grass is not as green as the other side, then we have an opportunity to water it. In other words, we can create our atmosphere in any which way we want it. We have an opportunity to assert ourselves to make things better in our lives and the lives of others. If we can't find an opportunity, then we must create an opportunity to nurture our well-being. For us to create something, we must move or act to make something happen. We must water the ground where we stand.

August 13

Adjusting a Sail

"I can't change the direction of the wind, but I can adjust my sails to always reach my destination." — Jimmy Dean[189]

*C*hange can feel like an impossible feat to do. However, a small change can do wonders in our life. A slight reorientation to our situation can make all the difference in the world to how we handle things. Life is already difficult. We don't have to make an alternation a huge event. It is better to start things small. It is easier to manage our lives when things are smaller. As long as we live, we will adjust our situation accordingly. Adjustment is another thing we do because it is part of life. Adjusting to a new situation means we are accepting the challenge. We're willing to put ourselves out when we feel it's necessary.

August 14

Life Is a Matter of Moments

"Life isn't a matter of milestones, but of moments."— Rose Kennedy[190]

*M*ilestones are meaningless without moments. It is the moments we remember when we make a milestone in our lives. We have moments of struggles, moments of successes, moments of frustrations, and also moments of failures. We have experienced all types of moments. These moments make us what we are today as we persevere. Those moments become our foundation we can build on for the next level of our self-development. It is all right to strive for a goal, but it is also the moments that make our goals meaningful and worth doing. We experience moments in the here and now and not necessarily in the future. We can experience touch and smells as long as we are present at the moment.

August 15

Run on the Right Track

"Even if you are on the right track, you'll get run over if you just sit there." — Will Rogers[191]

*I*t is not easy to stay on the right track, let alone sit there while waiting for something to happen. We can't afford to wait for something to happen, because if something were to happen, then how do we know we will be ready for it? We will be more ready if we act before an opportunity drops on our lap than if we don't take action. We will likely make mistakes, and we must give ourselves room for mistakes as that's how we learn about life. If we want to sit idle, then we can sit idle for a good reason. If we want to act, then we can act for a good reason. What we do is an expression of ourselves. We all want a satisfying experience when we express ourselves to the world. We want to feel useful and purposeful in what we do.

August 16

We're Different People Then

> "It's no use going back to yesterday, because I
> was a different person then."
> — Lewis Carroll, Alice in Wonderland[192]

That's one of the reasons we long for yesterday because we want to experience how things were then. We indeed had some good times, but we forget that we had some difficult times in our past as well. We were different people then because since then we have added new experiences and those experiences have changed us over time. Today we have different needs and desires. What was important then is different from what is important to us today. It is no use looking back at the past through today's lenses for something we want today. Our lives change over time whether that's our tastes in things or our values as we learn to get older physically and psychologically. We hope that we're getting wiser as time passes.

August 17

Your Self-Respect Blossoms

"Do something to allow your self-respect to blossom." — David Viscott[193]

It is important to nurture our self-respect. When we nurture self-respect, our self-esteem increases. However, self-doubt is one of the quickest ways to lower our self-esteem that in turn affects our self-respect. When an opportunity comes our way we can take advantage of it because we believe we deserve it. We believe we deserve an opportunity because we know we worked so hard to get to where we are now and we're ready to take it. We earn self-respect. We can be our worse enemy or our best advocate when it comes to choosing to build our self-respect or not. No one can lower our self-esteem unless we allow it. Self-respect gives us the privilege to express ourselves by doing what we find important to us.

August 18

Meaningful Past with Friends

> "Meaning is not what you start with but what you end up with." — Peter Elbow[194]

*T*he struggles and challenges are what we start with that give us meaning in the end. It is, even more, meaningful when we struggle together and help support each other to get through it. It is those memories we tell our story or reminisce about something we did in our past. When there are two or more of us reminiscing the past together, we collaborate and compare memories. One person may recall something we have forgotten. They recall a memory that was long forgotten about because it was more meaningful to them and how it's impacted their lives the most. As we reminisce, we re-experience the memory as though the event happened yesterday. We're re-establishing a special bond that we developed many years ago when we reminisce together.

August 19

Hold Head High

"Never bend your head. Always hold it high.
Look the world straight in the eye."
— Helen Keller[195]

*I*t is difficult to experience confidence when we keep our heads bent. However, if we hold our head high with confidence, we then will experience confidence and that others will see that and want to be around us. When we look at the world straight in the eye, we're engaging the world. We're freer when we're participants in the world instead of bystanders. If we're constantly looking down, we won't know what direction to take next. We built our confidence through the goals we set and met. We see that we build a foundation when we look back later at our work. Our foundation is our proof to ourselves that we can do what we thought about what we can't do before.

August 20

Jump, then Our Wings Unfold

"Jump, and you will find out how to unfold
your wings as you fall." — Ray Bradbury[196]

Sometimes we have to jump before we
could ever think about what we're getting
ourselves into when we leave our comfort zone.
As we jump, we're forced to use every brain ca-
pacity we have and every experience we have
for us to unfold our wings and learn how to fly
and to land properly. That's where we will find
our excitement and create meaningful experiences when we jump into something. It is about
taking risks. When we're taking risks, we're
defining who we are as a person. Growth happens when we take risks. Taking risks is life-
changing experiences and memories we can take
with us. As we recall our past adventures
through our memories, we can re-experience
them anytime we want.

August 21

Let It Rain

> *"The best thing one can do when it's raining is to let it rain."*
> — Henry Wadsworth Longfellow[197]

*W*e have to let things happen because things will somehow work itself out. Letting go implies accepting what we can't control. A rainy day is temporary. We may want the sunshine over rainy days. However, if we're in a drought, we would welcome rain because water maintains life. A sunny day is appreciated when it's been raining all day. So, it is better to get something out of a situation than lamenting about it. Perhaps we can learn to be part of the solution. A positive attitude can be useful in a difficult situation. We can better handle life when we just let it rain.

August 22

Don't Stop, Keep Going

"It does not matter how slowly you go as long as you do not stop." — Confucius[198]

*J*ust because someone is ahead of us doesn't mean we have to catch up with them. We all have our own pace in life. We all have different speeds in life too. We don't need to make comparisons. It is about us competing with ourselves, not with the other person. Since we have our own pace, then we don't have to rush things along. We don't stop doing until completion. We don't stop doing, because it is hard. We don't stop because it is a struggle. We can endure what's ahead of us as long as we don't stop prematurely. It is hard to start something new, it is harder to maintain something new, and the hardest is to complete something new. Our regrets are born out of our unfinished projects. But if we take our time doing things, then there will be fewer headaches in the end.

August 23

Change Your World

> "Change your thoughts and you change your world." — Norman Vincent Peale[199]

We see the world through our thoughts. If we see the world with our thoughts, then it is our world we see. Our thoughts can distort reality. We interpret the world based on our previous experiences. Therefore, our minds automatically fill in the gaps without testing our assumptions. There will always be some degree of distortions when we see the world. "The map is not the territory."   Since the map is not the territory, then we can change our map any way we want. Communication is the key to testing our assumptions and verifying facts. We alter our world when our assumptions are challenged. When our world expands, we see clearly that we don't have to overreact toward things. We just accept what is and use what we have already to move our world.

August 24

Look at Your Darkness

"Your willingness to look at your darkness is what empowers you to change."
— Iyanla Vanzant[200]

*J*ust as it is difficult to listen to a recording of our voice, it is difficult looking at our foibles or weaknesses. Sometimes we do things out of our weaknesses and then later regret that we did them. We play the denial game on others and ourselves. We deny the fact that what we're doing can have a big effect on us. The conscious learnings eventually move to the back of our minds. Our learnings and behaviors become automatic. Most things we do become second nature and that we don't think about them. We're designed this way so we can do more than one thing simultaneously. But once we begin to observe how we respond to different situations, we then can alter our behavior.

August 25

Follow Your Passion

"Follow your passion, and success will follow you." — Terri Guillemets[201]

*W*e're not looking for success when we follow our passion. When we follow our passion, we don't mind the great labor it takes to want it because we already have what it takes to get it. When our days are up, we follow our passion, and when our days are down, we continue still to follow our passion. We follow our passion because we enjoy doing it. We follow our passion because it gives us satisfaction and purpose. Our success is meaningful when we follow our passion. We can do without success because our passion is our driving force to continue doing it. Sometimes success can stifle our passion if we're not careful. We follow our passion because we like doing it not because we can be successful in doing it. Our passion always remains when our success leaves us.

August 26

The Motivating Factor

"Poverty was the greatest motivating factor in my life." — Jimmy Dean[202]

*W*hen stripped to almost nothing, there is something inside us that motivates us somehow to change our situation. Self-reliance grows out of life or death situations. There are times in our lives we had to hustle to get above the red line. We must learn to trust ourselves to do what is necessary to pull ourselves up out of a well. Self-preservation is a powerful motivator when we're between a rock and hard place because we are forced to make decisions quickly and to do what must be done to get out of our predicament. There is no room for procrastination when time is of the essence. We hear many success stories about individuals who've gone from rags to riches. A common denominator that motivated these individuals to do something that made a difference in their lives was an immediate threat to self-preservation.

August 27

The Beginning of Happiness

"Knowledge of what is possible is the beginning of happiness" — George Santayana[203]

We're unhappy when we get stuck in a rut. If we see no possibility of getting out of a rut, then our mind is closed for new ideas. For us to get out of a rut, we have to see things in a new light. Ideas come after processing the knowledge we have learned. New ideas help us to expand our minds to see what's possible. Knowledge is power because it will reveal to us something that we haven't heard before. We don't have to be stuck doing the same thing every day. We can rearrange our routine, so we don't have to stay stuck for long. Rearranging our routines fragment the old pattern so we can produce new patterns and new behaviors. New behaviors bring new possibility thus the beginning of happiness.

August 28

Tie a Knot, and Hang On

> "When you reach the end of your rope, tie a
> knot in it and hang on."
> — Franklin Roosevelt[204]

*W*e all experienced days when nothing goes right. Our patience was tested when everything decided to break around the same time. We just want the day to be over before we scream at the top of our lungs. We can only fix things one thing at a time. We can't fix things simultaneously. Although we could be in a jam, we can always take steps back to see the forest for us to figure out a plan to get ourselves out of a jam. When we take steps back, this will help us to find some clarity to see if there are options available to remedy the situation. We won't be able to fix everything because problems will always arise. All we can do is take one problem at a time and hope for the best and keep our heads high.

August 29

Thank You

"Praise the bridge that carried you over."
— George Colman[205]

*W*hen we become mindful of what we can be thankful for, then our problems become smaller. We can be thankful for the simplest thing like breathing the air. Breathing air is basic and life-saving because we can't live without it. Simple things can make another person's day brighter. Putting in the time and effort is always worth doing when another person thanks us for it. Life is good when we're thankful. Our attitude becomes positive when we're counting the good things that are already happening in our lives. Counting the good things that are already happening can lift us out of our worries, stresses, and frustrations. Things begin to turn around when we begin to see that we're thankful. It is worth a few moments to recall what those good things are in our lives.

August 30

Make a Way

"Either I will find a way, or I will make one."
— Philip Sidney[206]

If we search long enough eventually, we may find a way. If we can't find a way, then we can create a way for us and for those who are looking for a way. Either finding a way or making a way takes determination and a willingness to learn what we're after. In other words, if we see no opportunity, then we must reconsider creating opportunities. It is better to leave our minds open to new things. If we find ourselves not willing to do because it is uncomfortable, then we will never find out our potential. There is always some level of discomfort when we do something outside the uncharted territory. However, an opportunity is where we've hadn't gone or done before.

August 31

Value Upon Yourself

"If you really put a small value upon yourself, rest assured that the world will not raise your price."— Unknown[207]

*W*e're just as important as the next person. How we value ourselves determines how the world values us. Self-respect increases how we value ourselves. When we accomplish something life-changing for us, we can pat ourselves on the back and be proud. Small accomplishments can also make us proud of ourselves. Everyone has disappointments just as everyone has accomplishments. Although we're not defined by our accomplishments, but by how we see ourselves. We don't have to be so hard on ourselves. Our patience is the most important virtue that we could have for ourselves because we will need it during challenging times. It starts with us to rediscover how valuable we are and that we can contribute to the world.

September 1

Led by Your Dreams

"Don't be pushed by your problems; be led by your dreams." — Unknown[208]

*W*e all have problems. We all have dreams. Our problems don't have to interfere with our dreams. Our dreams don't have to interfere with our problems. We must respect the two things.

It is all right for our dreams to lead us anywhere we can imagine. We would rather be led by our dreams than to be pushed around by our problems. We can use our imagination to solve some of our problems if we can. When we are thinking about our problems, we are looking down at the ground but when we're dreaming, we are looking up at the bright stars at night.

We will always have our problems, and we will always have our dreams. Dreams are the opportunities we make for ourselves to fulfill. Where we dream is where our hearts will follow.

September 2

The Mightier Conquers Self

"He who conquers others is strong; He who conquers himself is mighty." — Lao Tzu[209]

*W*e tend to want to conquer others because we think that's the source of the problem. If we don't wield our power, someone else will. If we want our control back, then we must use our power. We must learn how to conquer ourselves. Therefore, our focus has to be on ourselves, not somebody else for us to change. It is an illusion to suggest that we can make someone change. We have free will. Since we have free will, we can decide what we want to do, how we should react to an external situation. When we don't feel like doing something difficult, then it is time to conquer self. When we don't want to get up in the morning, then it is time to conquer self. When we put up with it and then do it to completion, we are conquering ourselves.

September 3

From Good to Better

"Don't be afraid of change. You may lose something good, but you may gain something better." — Unknown[210]

The first thing we think of when making a change is that we may lose something good. The reality is that we will lose something good. But for us to move forward on life's journey we must make some changes. The change is already inevitable as it is taking place right now. Change requires us to make an extra effort in learning a new skill and learning a new routine. Therefore, in learning something new, we gain something even better than we've done before. During this process of change and learning, we gain confidence in ourselves. There is nothing better than having confidence in one's self.

September 4

Feel Today Strong Tomorrow

"The pain you feel today will be the strength you feel tomorrow." — Unknown[211]

*N*o one likes to experience pain whether that's emotional or physical. However, physical pain is our body's way of telling us to pay attention and to make the pain go away. Psychological pain, which we all experience, is, for the most part, normal reactions to difficult situations. Pain is temporary if we let ourselves feel the emotion that's causing the pain. We can get our needed strength from all the pain we've experienced because we've had gone through the pain. Sometimes, we mask our pain through our anger because we don't want anyone to know that we're in pain. Anger makes us feel powerful while experiencing pain makes us feel vulnerable and weak. In truth, expressing our pain means letting go thus releasing energy. It takes a lot of energy to hold energy in.

September 5

A Day Closer

> "I may not be there yet, but I'm closer than I
> was yesterday." — Author Unknown[212]

*W*hen we work on our dreams each day, it is another day closer to fulfilling our dreams. The times we want to give up are the times we have the opportunity to look again at our dreams for inspiration and motivation. Fulfilling a dream is never a smooth drive; there are always bumpy roads we have to go through. Those bumpy roads are there to fine-tune our new skills and to build character to prepare us to handle things better in our future. With a dream, there is a purpose in our lives we want to fulfill. A dream without a purpose is just a dream. However, a dream with a purpose makes everything we do to fulfill our dreams have meaning. We don't have to make a wish; instead, we can make a dream come true if we continue to persist.

September 6

The Next Chapter of Life

> "You can't start the next chapter of your life if
> you keep re-reading the last one."
> — Unknown[213]

$\mathcal{H}$olding on to the past is the very foundation as to why we can't move forward. Letting go of the past also means letting go of old ideas. Some of our ideas can be outdated and that we need an upgrade. For us to move forward in life, we need an upgrade. Getting an education is always useful when we need to learn something for us to move up in life. We never stop improving our lives as long as we live each day. Each day we learn something even when that learning is outside our awareness. We're always picking up something. The learning may be useless, or it may be useful to apply to our daily lives.

September 7

Action Feeds Courage

"Thinking will not overcome fear, but action will."— W. Clement Stone[214]

*T*hinking is the very thing that causes fear. Doubting is a mental exercise that preoccupies our attention away from our goal. The mental energy is being misused until we redirect our energy back to what's important. If we act despite our fear, then we will realize that we can discover what things we can do without feeling inadequate. Our action is a way for us to build self-confidence, which we will need, the most of when we start to tackle things we only dream about. Action creates an atmosphere of feeling in control of oneself instead of allowing fear to control us. Our action discharges fear eventually if we allow it to happen. Fears should be reserved for self-preservation when we need to be alert to life and death situations. Action feeds on our abilities while fear feeds on our limitations.

September 8

Nurture Our Mind

"Nurture your mind with great thoughts, for you will never go any higher than you think."
— Benjamin Disraeli[215]

*O*ur thoughts have a big influence on us than we think. If we say to ourselves that we won't get better doing this or that, then we will find evidence to prove to ourselves that we won't get better doing this or that thing. However, if we say to ourselves that we will get better doing this or that as long as we hang in there, then we will begin to find self-proof that we're getting better doing this or that thing. If we want something but don't want to do the work and expect to get it somehow, then we're deluded ourselves. Working hard on something won't be guaranteed instant success but the possibility is greater for success. It is in our thinking that will take us to where ever we want to go in life if we nurture the mind with great thoughts. Self-doubt likes to creep its head sometimes. Self-doubt is just a way to let us know that we're going to uncharted territory and that's all.

September 9

Who Are You?

"Believing in our hearts that who we are is enough is the key to a more satisfying and balanced life."— Ellen Sue Stern[216]

*W*hat does it mean to know who we are? We perceived the world through our filters. The filters are unique to each of us. Therefore, the way we see the world is truly a reflection of our background and our personality. It is ourselves that we need to impress the most, not others. We have a relationship with ourselves. We sometimes are harder on ourselves than others. We can be our worse enemy or our best advocate. If we seemed to be disappointed about life, then it may be about how disappointed we are about ourselves. For us to feel more satisfaction and have a balanced life, we must first embrace ourselves for what we are, which includes the good, and the bad. It is better to laugh often at ourselves than to beat ourselves up because we didn't do something the way we expected it to be.

September 10

Fulfilled Life

"Remember that sometimes not getting what you want is a wonderful stroke of luck." — Dalai Lama[217]

*W*e all have needs, wants, and desires we want to fulfill. The problem is we sometimes want them now. Although the world is fast-paced, we don't have to have things right away. Sometimes it is good to regroup and ask ourselves, do we need this thing or that thing in our lives? Can we live without fulfilling a desire or getting something that we think we need? Those things we have already in our lives are unfulfilling; either we no longer interact with them or perhaps we have this need to fill some void in our lives. We all have voids in our lives some are bigger than others. However, we will always have some void. Nothing can fill a void. However, we're strong enough to live a fulfilling life with an unfilled void.

September 11

Remembrance of 911

*Y*esterday was the day of reflection and remembrance of 911. Today is the day we live for those loved-ones who died tragically. They will remain in our hearts for the rest of our lives. When we reflect on those that lost their lives, we're revisiting that moment in time. We got to stay strong for them. The moment in time changed the rest of our lives forever. It reminds us of what matters in life. We hope now that we have a better perspective on things.

September 12

Retreat to Our Sanctuary

"Within you there is a stillness and a sanctuary to which you can retreat at any time and be yourself." — Hermann Hesse[218]

For us to sit quietly for a moment or two, we must let go of the external events that are happening around us. When external things are stressing us out, then it is okay to retreat. The benefits of retreating are to help us to renew our bodies and reset our minds so we can have a better handle on things. When we renew our bodies, we have more energy, and when we reset our minds, we have a clearer understanding of things. Our sanctuary is within us where we can be ourselves and feel freer to contemplate and we just sit still until we're ready to return to the world. We can't be most effective when we're burned out and unfocused but after some time away, we want to return to do the work as the world welcome us back.

September 13

We Make the Conditions Perfect

"Do not wait until the conditions are perfect to begin. Beginning makes the conditions perfect."— Alan Cohen[219]

*W*aiting for the perfect condition is another excuse or distraction to keep us from doing what we may perceive to be a difficult task. If we perceive the task to be difficult, then we're thinking too much about it. Our thinking has been misdirected to something useless, and because it keeps us from moving forward. Instead, we ought to use our thinking while working on the task itself. We need our minds to see what works and what doesn't work and then use what works to further our progress. Just as Alan Cohen says in the above quote — the time we start is the time that the conditions begin to shape up into something we can work with. Seemingly, things begin to fall into place all by themselves after we begin.

September 14

Our Determination to Learn

"If you're not willing to learn, no one can help you. If you're determined to learn, no one can stop you." — Unknown[220]

The one thing that no one can take from us is our willingness to learn. Learning increases our power. The power we need to be assertive in life so we can make decisive choices. Ultimately for us to help ourselves, we must spend some time learning things to build self-confidence. We are teachable beings as long as we're open-minded to new things. When we're determining to learn, then we have an opportunity to make things happen in our life that hasn't happened before. Our unwillingness to learn increases our fear while our determination to learn alleviates our fears. New learning breaks up rigidity and biases. We all have some biases about something we know very little. When we learn new things we learn new ways to approach new things. Learning helps us to go beyond what we've learned yesterday. For us to move forward we must learn new things.

September 15

Enjoying Your Own Life

> *"Enjoy your own life without comparing it with that of another."*
> — Marquis de Condorcet[221]

*W*e don't know what goes on behind closed doors of someone's life. All that we know is what the individual wants us to know about them. Instead, we can enjoy our own life because we know what makes us happy and what makes us unhappy. Comparing our life with another just implies that we aren't satisfied with our own life. We don't need what the other person has for us to have a fulfilled life. Besides, we aren't that other person. What makes one person happy is very different than what makes another person happy. We just have to return to what made us smile originally and do more of those things. So, let us stop looking outward to find tranquility but instead find it within because every one of us is different and we know ourselves. It's like comparing an apple to an orange. The orange is no better than the apple as they both have their own pleasant texture, smell and taste.

September 16

Done in Steps

"Step by step and the thing is done."
— Charles Atlas[222]

*I*f we just take one step at a time, we will get to our destinations. All it takes are steps for us to complete things. Each step we take is a step closer to our dreams of becoming more real. We take the first step, then the second, and so on, and then it is up to us to complete the final step, when it becomes no longer an idea but something we can touch. We may not see our whole path, but we will continue taking steps. If we're stepping in the wrong direction we can always temporarily step back until we see a better path where our hearts will lead us. It is better to start with baby steps first to help build up our confidence in making more bold and direct steps.

September 17

The Choice That Makes Us

"We all make choices, but in the end our choices make us." — Andrew Ryan[223]

*W*hatever choice we make in life always has the potential to change us somehow. We become molded by them. We have made many choices up to now. We make choices every day without thinking. We know through trial and error, generally speaking, as to what choices are useful and what choices are not.

There were times in our past that we made life-changing choices and there will be more in our future. Usually, these life-changing choices are when we're going through some transitional period in our life that everyone experiences.

We've made the wrong choices and the right choices. We will continue to make the wrong and right choices throughout our lifetime.

We have to make choices in our lives to continue to move along in the world. We can't live without choices.

September 18

Risk with Fear Then Live with Confidence

"Risk comes from not knowing what you're doing." — Warren Buffett[224]

*I*f we don't take risks, then we take away our choices. When we take away our choices, we feel stuck. And fear controls when we don't take risks. So fear can deceive us into believing that there are no choices. For us to overcome fear we must go through fear. Our fears don't have to control our actions. Instead, we can see fear as a positive response to a new situation.

We can use our fears as an asset instead of as a liability. Our fear is just a barometer that we're about to take some risks that are outside our comfort zone. Sometimes we won't know what we're doing until we do it a few more times until we feel confident in ourselves doing it which eventually lessens the fear. Fear doesn't have to be used as a crutch but can be used to remind ourselves that we're about to grow outside our comfort zone.

September 19

Educating a Willing Mind

> "Education's purpose is to replace an empty
> mind with an open one."
> — Malcolm S. Forbes[225]

*E*ducation stimulates our imagination. Education gets us to look at things differently. If we want to know something, we get ourselves educated. Our minds can come to understand if we allow ourselves to be willing to learn about what we don't understand. Fear can sometimes keep us in the dark when we need an open mind. Education is the first initial process for opening up the mind. We see more possibilities when our minds are open to things while a closed mind sees no possibilities, then, therefore no opportunities. Opportunities grow out of possibilities when the mind is open for new adventures. Education informs us and helps us to think critically about a situation so we can make better-informed decisions. Education helps us to expand our horizon so we can see more of the vastness of life can offer.

September 20

When Worry Saps Today's Joy

"Worry never robs tomorrow of its sorrow. It only saps today of its joy."— Leo Buscaglia[226]

*Y*esterday we worried about today and we see that today we had no reason to worry but an opportunity to experience joy. Worrying takes us away from the present. We needn't use our time worrying when we have the opportunity today to be happy. We can be grateful when nothing occurs happen that would cause us to worry. If we know we have only a finite time to live our lives, then why wasted on worrying about something that we have no control over. Instead, we have more control over what we can do today and we can hope for a better tomorrow. Today is the present that brings us joy into our lives. Today is our present because we have another opportunity to start a new chapter. We have this today to fill up with different experiences.

September 21

Against the Wind

> "Kites rise highest against the wind, not with it." — Churchill[227]

$\mathscr{I}$t is difficult to walk up a steep hill but not impossible. It may take some time and struggle but we needn't stop because we will soon get to the top. Likewise, most of our difficulties reside in our heads. We anticipate that every task we do will take great labor. But not every task we do will be as difficult as we think. The most difficult thing about doing a new task is to begin the task. Of course, there will be some level of difficulties but not to the point where we delay starting a project. We can always divide the tasks into small parts so that they can be more manageable. We do get stronger and pick up things faster each time when we push ourselves beyond the difficulty. Hard work is truly character building.

September 22

When Moments Become Memories

*"Sometimes you will never know the value of
a moment until it becomes a memory."*
— Dr. Seuss[228]

*I*t is quite an experience when we reminisce, especially with friends and/or
family who share the same experience. During
this time of reminiscing, there is always someone in the group that will say, "Those were the
good old days," or "Those were innocent times."
These quotes are pointing to experiences we've
had over time. They are shared experiences. The
shared experiences become valuable as the years
go by because they are special moments in time.
We have eventful milestones in our lives that
somehow changed the course of our lives. Those
are the things we cherish most as we get older.
And there were things in our past that seemed at
the time insignificant but are now significant. It
is better to not take things for granted today because they will be missed tomorrow.

September 23

Peaceful Thoughts

"You are today where your thoughts have brought you; you will be tomorrow where your thoughts take you." — James Allen[229]

*O*ur thoughts are what influence our mood, feelings, and actions. We are our thoughts. Our thoughts are the extension of our personality. What we say and do is the product of our thoughts. We think about our thoughts when we're alone and they keep us company. We take our thoughts with us wherever we go. We may not have control over our thoughts, but we can think of other pleasant thoughts. Our memory can influence our thoughts a great deal. We can think of a peaceful moment from our memory and then be filled with peaceful thoughts. Experiencing serenity is the product of peaceful thoughts. Therefore, amid of chaos, we can experience serenity through what we imagined because of peaceful thoughts.

September 24

How Far You've Come

"Always concentrate on how far you've come,
rather than how far you have left to go."
— Unknown[230]

When we get discouraged, it would be a good reminder for us to look back on how far we've come to lift our spirits. When we see how far we've come, we then can get an understanding that those times in our past were struggles but we went through them. We hope that we will get through today's struggles as well. We wouldn't be where we are today; if it weren't for our past struggles. Life will always have its ups and downs. So, when life is up, we can be glad and when life is down, we can be thankful. It is our hopes and dreams that keep us going clear into the future.

September 25

You Are Most Powerful

> "When you do not seek or need approval, you are at your most powerful."
> — Caroline Myss[231]

*T*hen the question is raised as to why are we at our most powerful when we no longer need or seek the approval of others? We don't need to rely on others when we can rely on ourselves for our approval. There are no longer internal conflicts about what we think versus what the other person thinks about us. We become our person when we make our own decisions as to what we want to do in our lives and then carry them out until completion. We no longer have to second-guess the decisions we make in our lives. We have only one life to live between now and dead; we might as well live it to how we want because our contentment depends on it. Life is too short, or too long to wait on someone's approval. If we still need to seek someone's approval for our decisions, then we need more maturing to do. More maturing means being comfortable with our own decisions.

September 26

Shed Light on the Real You

"You'll never know who you are unless you shed who you pretend to be."
— Vironika Tugaleva[232]

*W*hen we're pretending to be someone else, we're wasting our time and energy when we could just be ourselves. We don't have to hide behind something we're not. We can trust being ourselves and allow others to decide if they like us or not. It's not fair to others when we don't show our real selves. It takes a lot of energy to pretend to be someone else. That energy can be used to pursue our dreams. Dreams are an extension of us. We express ourselves through our dreams and goals, and that allows us to be who we are. As we continue to pursue our dreams and to fulfill them, we will discover our full potential and discover more of our purpose and how we can contribute to the world so others may benefit. The real person will draw others and others can see through pretenses. When we're pretentious we're not accepting of ourselves. No one is without faults or imperfections. Let us accept everything about us and just be.

September 27

Trust the Process

"Let go of the need to control the outcome.
Trust the process. Trust your Intuition. Trust
yourself." — Unknown[233]

*H*ow come we want to be rewarded so
quickly? We have missed the point if
our attention is focused on the outcome. We
learn the most during the process of getting to
the outcome. Learning has its own reward. As
long as we proceed with the process the outcome is inevitable. When we don't see clearly
what we do next in a process, then it is time to
rely more on our intuition or hunches. The feeling in our gut is based on past experiences and
what we've already learned from the process so
far. Therefore, we must trust ourselves in this
process since we've been in sync with what's
happening around us. If our hunch is incorrect,
then we at least know that approach is not going
to lead us to the outcome we were expecting. It's
trial and error.

September 28

Outside the Comfort Zone

"All progress takes place outside the comfort zone." — Michael John Bobak[234]

*G*etting out of our comfort zone sometimes evoke fears and doubts in us. However, we forget that getting out of our comfort zone is an opportunity for us to grow and expand ourselves. Every day we will experience some kind of discomfort here and there and we have learned how to adjust. When it is something new for us our anxiety and/or stress levels may increase because we don't know what to expect. We're scrambling to find and learn the new pattern of things. We're afraid we may make a mistake. However, we will make mistakes as we continue learning. We may need to get up earlier than we're used to. We may have to stay up later studying up on things just to get familiar with a project, which may include some training. There will be times when we will experience resistance to continue on a task and that is the time that we must place ourselves outside of our comfort zone. As we continue to learn the ins and outs of things our discomfort will decrease.

September 29

Live Your Life

"Live your life and forget your age. "
— Norman Vincent Peale[235]

*Y*es, there are some limitations when it comes to age sometimes. However, it doesn't mean we stop dreaming and living our lives. If we're able to walk, talk, hear, see, and have a functional mind, then we still can continue to do things we enjoy the most with a purpose. It's never too late to do most things in life. Our age doesn't have to be the barometer for what we can and can't do. We don't have to allow societal pressures to dictate how we live our lives because of our background, age, or anything that perceived to be a limitation. Life is meant for living no matter what the age. We can learn from individuals that are younger and older than we're and they can learn from us because we're a community of people with a variety of influences like education, art, business, etc.

September 30

People Who Believe in Themselves

"People believe in those who believe in themselves." — Unknown[236]

*W*e're drawn to those who have self-confidence and feel comfortable in their own skin. Self-confidence is earned over time. For us, to gain confidence we must allow ourselves to experience life. We all have a relationship with ourselves. When we give a person our word that we will do something and we follow through with it, we're building confidence in the relationship. However, if we give ourselves our word that we will do something but don't follow through with it, and then we will lose confidence in ourselves and we leave ourselves with disappointments. Our relationship with ourselves is just as important as our relationship with others. If we're willing to say yes to others but say no to ourselves, we're dismissing ourselves with disrespect. When our main concern is to please others, we're neglecting what we want in life. If we want to win ourselves over, then we must start respecting ourselves by following through with our word. When we follow through with our word, then we begin to believe in ourselves.

October 1

Life Goes On

"In three words I can sum up everything I've learned about life: it goes on."
— **Robert Frost**[237]

It is okay to take breaks or to retreat. It is important to do these things to prevent burnout. Sometimes we think that if we're not there where things are happening, the world or our world will crumble apart. That's so untrue. Life will always continue when we're long gone. That is our hope, to know that it is true that life does continue. So, what does that mean to us to know that life will go on with or without us? It means that we can slow down our pace; we can live moment-by-moment enjoying life because life will take care of itself. We are part of a bigger picture; we're not the big picture. Knowing that we're not the big picture can bring us some relief instead of a heavy burden.

October 2

Only I Can Change

"Only I can change my life. No one can do it
for me." — Carol Burnett[238]

*I*f change is going to make a difference in
our lives, then it is up to us to make the
change. Making our change builds self-confidence. It is all right to ask for guidance and/or
have someone hold us accountable to our goals.
On the other hand, we can't change another person's life. They must make their changes themselves. We can't depend on another to change
our lives and others can't depend on us to
change theirs. We can only challenge each other
if we decide beforehand to hold each other li-
able. We have the power inside us to make a
difference. Therefore, we don't have to wait for
opportunities to transform our lives we can start
today by making preparations. Making preparations is doing our research, developing our
skills, and getting actively involved with others
with the same interests.

October 3

What Matters Most Is Today

"Every morning we are born again. What we do today is what matters most." — Buddha[239]

*W*hat we do today is what matters most because the action can only work in the present, not in the past or the future. In the past we can only reflect while looking at the future we can only plan and anticipate an outcome of some sort. We retire at night, we sleep until dawn, and then we rise to start a new day. Regrets get smaller each day when we take action. A new day is another opportunity to do great work in our lives. When we do look back on what we have done, we can smile and be grateful and then we can look into the future and we can be hopeful for more days ahead. We can only live one day at a time. The regrets of the past and the anxieties of the future are nullified when we act today.

October 4

An Unconscious Request

"Never go to sleep without a request to your subconscious." — Thomas Edison[240]

$\mathcal{I}$t is interesting that Thomas Edison the American inventor understood the concept of the subconscious or unconscious mind. That our unconscious can solve a problem or get us where we want to go just by requesting something reasonable to our unconscious. Our unconscious mind may not be solving a problem or recalling a memory right away, but it will continue working on it long after the request. We just have to pay close attention when our unconscious mind is ready to reveal to us consciously the results it came up with. Although Sigmund Freud understood the subconscious mind to be filled with repressed emotions and symbolisms, Thomas Edison saw our subconscious mind more in a positive light to be used as a tool to assist in resolutions. Both men lived in the same era. Both men have used their ideas and changed our world into what it is today.

October 5

Push through with Persistence

"Persistent people begin their success where others end in failure." — Edward Eggleston[241]

In other words, we don't have to give up; we should stay with it because the day we give up might be the day we succeed. Persistence is moving through trial times when we want to surrender. Persistence is learning how to be comfortable in an uncomfortable situation. Persistence teaches us how to handle our struggles, our battles within us. Persistence is not being afraid of obstacles. As long as we see that persistence is helping us to make further progress in our quest to succeed. Failure doesn't mean that we have given up, instead is just a milestone to success. Persistence is our determination to move uphill despite a windy day. Persistent people are willing to learn from their mistakes and make sacrifices. Great labor is inevitable if we want to succeed in life.

October 6

Blessings In Disguise

"What seems to us as bitter trials are often
blessings in disguise." — Oscar Wilde[242]

Sometimes, things fall in our laps unexpectedly when we think we're not ready
for them. Those are the times when we experience trepidations because we aren't sure if we
can do it. We have to learn as quickly as possible
and sometimes be thrown to wolves and see
how we can handle things while we're under a
lot of pressure to perform. Some of us can do
well when we're pressed to do something im-
mediately and while some of us don't. We're
tested during those times so we can discover
how well we can deal. It is a blessing when we
find out that we do have the inner strength to
get through and that our abilities and our latent
potentials emerge for this occasion. If we don't
push beyond our limits to grow the universe
somehow will push us. Some of us need a push
to do something every once in a while if we
don't push ourselves.

October 7

When Dreams Come True

"The best way to make your dreams come true is to wake up." — Paul Valéry[243]

*D*reams can bring us hope for new possibilities. But, if we want to see those dreams are possible, then we must wake up and make them real in our lives. That's the only way to find out if our dreams are possible to do while awake. We live in the here and now not in our dreams. There is no need for us to waste time daydreaming when we can use our time making our dreams come true. Perhaps dreams are meant for sleep not while we're awake. Let us stop dreaming and start living our lives the way we want and stop wishing our lives away while awake. Dreams come true when we do the work. The work is our opportunity for growth so why wait now when we have the time. If we hear a faint nagging voice from the back our head saying that we can do better than this, then we ought to listen to it and then do better with our lives.

October 8

Be More of Value

"Strive not to be a success, but rather to be of value." — Albert Einstein[244]

$\int$ uccess is more about us, and value is more about others. When we were kids, we all wanted to grow up to be something and be successful at it. That means spending time working on ourselves to become what we see ourselves doing in the future. We don't have to perceive success as something bad or good but as something we want to do and have the desire for doing it. Just as we want others to be of value for us and also the same rings true that we want to be of value for others. That's very important to us because we want to somehow feel useful for another person. When we want to be of value for others, we're thinking about how best to serve them instead of thinking about how can I be successful in this or that. We can use our experiences from our success and be of more value toward others.

October 9

Accept Life As Is

"Surrender to what is. Say 'yes' to life—and see
how life suddenly starts working for you
rather than against you."— Eckhart Tolle[245]

*A*s we accept life as it is, we no longer
have to be resistant toward it. When
we have an urge to control the things
we cannot control, the things we have no control
over don't necessarily mean we have no control
over our lives. We just have to distinguish what
things we do have control over from what things
we don't have control over. Once we know the
difference then it is easier to surrender to what
is. We don't have to fall victim to the things we
have no control over but to continue to be proactive in the things we do have control over. If we
fall victim to the things that we have no control
over, then we're distracting ourselves from being proactive. We are the author and the pilot of
our lives so we have the power to alter our
course. Things only become real to us when we
produce actions instead of producing lamenting
thoughts, which only produces inaction.

October 10

Practice Builds Confidence

> "An ounce of practice is worth tons of preaching." — Mahatma Gandhi[246]

Practicing has a way of building confidence. We may not have confidence in the beginning. However, as we practice a skill over and over we will get better than if we didn't practice at all. Practicing saves a lot of time. We do need some guidance from time to time. Once we're shown the proper way to do a skill, we then take over the rest in practice. We can practice alone or we can practice with others especially if they're practicing the same skill. This allows us to support each other and to challenge each other to grow further in our training. We learn much faster practicing than if someone was giving us tips and tricks on how to improve on our skills. Practicing a skill can be tedious, however, it will be well worth it at the end.

October 11

The Struggle Strengthens

*W*hen the possibility of our dream is becoming a reality, we shouldn't run the other way. It's easier to sabotage or delay our dreams than to continue pushing towards our dream. Making our dream a reality is like pushing a heavy load of bricks up a hill—it isn't easy. Nonetheless, it's nice to look back on our progress because that can motivate us to push harder and continue forward until we get to where we want to go. Success can also be hard to deal with because we've become accustomed to the struggle. The struggle to succeed becomes our purpose instead of meeting our goal we have set for ourselves, but the struggle can make us stronger for the next difficult task.

October 12

Crazy New Idea

> "Every really new idea looks crazy at
> first." — Abraham H. Maslow[247]

*I*t may seem to be implausible or coun-
terintuitive when we first hear of a new
idea because it might have come out of
a different context that we haven't experienced
before. Civilizations were built on crazy ideas. It
is always a risk to make a new idea into something real because we don't know what to expect. We don't know if the new idea will work
only if we test and then wait and see what happens. We will never know if the new ideas work
unless they're tested. As we're testing them, we
will learn and discover more ideas and most
importantly get an understanding as to how
new ideas will help in the long run. That's why
we brainstorm to look for other ways (new
ideas) to do things better and sufficiently.

October 13

Strengths, Setbacks and Progress

*"The beautiful things about setbacks is they
introduce us to our strengths."*
— Robin Sharma[248]

A setback is just another obstacle or delay
in our progress. When we experience a
setback, we find out not only what our weaknesses are but also our strengths. We just have to
use our strengths to get us through the obstacle
and not be distracted by our weaknesses. Setbacks can be opportunities to find out what
we're made of so we don't have to give up. We
ought to respect our strengths and understand
that everyone has weaknesses no one is immune
to setbacks. Setbacks are inevitable. Somehow,
we have this notion that progress moves in a
straight line going from point A to point B, but
the reality is that there are many dips and
falls and more dips and more falls. As long as
we continue to move forward, the dips and the
falls will not have any effects on our progress.
Our progress is built upon our strengths to
move through and around the setbacks slow and
steady.

October 14

Repeatedly Do

> "We are what we repeatedly do; excellence,
> then, is not an act but a habit." — Aristotle[249]

*T*he only act we need to begin is to start;
after that, we make repeats of the new
behaviors until they become a habit. When
habits are developed, then they become characteristics of our personality. It takes time for a
new behavior to develop into a habit. This is a
constant struggle because we want to stop when
we don't see quick results. Patience is also a key
to success or excellence because we have to allow ourselves the room for failure and to fall on
our faces and then get back up to start all over
again. After everything is said and done, then
we can look back on our work and appreciate
the effort we put into the work in a meaningful
way.

October 15

Think Less Feel More

*"Get out of your head and get into your heart.
Think less, feel more."* — Osho[250]

$\mathcal{W}$e're avoiding feeling pain when we find
ourselves intellectualizing trivia things.
Being stoic is only showing everyone else that
we don't have feelings, however, the truth is that
we have repressed feelings waiting to be felt.
When we learn to feel negative emotions, then
we can allow ourselves to feel positive ones like
joy. We're more connected with the world and
ourselves when we're connected with our feelings. Pain is a temporary stay when we start expressing the feeling especially to an individual
who caused us to hurt. There are no more
grudges when we let go of hurt feelings just by
expressing them. Feelings breathe color into our
world. No one is saying that we should not
think at all, but the quote above is saying that it
is better to feel more in our hearts, and think less
in our heads.

October 16

You Will Know How to Live

"As soon as you trust yourself, you will know
how to live."
— Johann Wolfgang von Goethe[251]

From birth until now, we have gone through many experiences. Wisdom comes from our experiences. Wisdom is the result of our experiences. Our abilities are the result of our experiences. So, if we combine both our wisdom and our abilities, then we will know how to live. However, we need to trust our wisdom and our abilities to live a decent life. Trust is relying on self to move forward even when we partially know the answers. We don't need all the answers to things before we proceed. We will find most of the answers along the way. Doubt is the opposite of trust. We're unsure when we doubt ourselves. Doubts are only thoughts and are unreal. So, let us allow ourselves to be entrusted with how we live our lives and not allow doubt to stop us from doing just that.

October 17

Overcoming Suffering

"The world is full of suffering. It is also full of overcoming it." — Helen Keller[252]

*I*t is good to know that we have people all over the world who are overcoming suffering and that gives us hope for those who are suffering. We want to believe that suffering is only temporary so that we have hope in overcoming our suffering. There are emotional and physical suffering to overcome. Life brings difficulties in our lives. Most of our difficulties are a transitioning period of our lives. Life is always constantly changing. And we're changing with life difficulties. No one is without difficulties whether we are rich or poor we still have to deal with what life brings to us. Suffering is part of life but it isn't the only part of life we should focus on. We move through our suffering because we must if we want to learn something about ourselves that we didn't know about.

October 18

Imperfection Is Okay to Be

**"When you stop expecting people to be perfect,
you can like them for who they are."
— Donald Miller[253]**

*W*hen we wish another person to behave a certain way, but to only be disappointed by his or her behaviors, then it is time for us to lower our expectations. We need to let go of those expectations and to let them be. We can only do our best and to accept our foibles and do not reflect our foibles on to another. Milton Erickson once said to a bride and groom to not give up on your faults, but instead, keep them because you're going to need them to understand your spouse's. That's a very powerful statement because we're forced to understand that everyone is imperfect one way or another and that each one of us has to struggle daily managing our imperfections. We're all in this together because no one is without faults.

October 19

If We Want Something New

"If you want something new, you have to stop doing something old." — Peter F. Drucker[254]

*R*outines are useful if we want to have predictability in our lives. However, doing the same things everyday can lose their meaning. Therefore, it is all right to do something new to add some spice to our lives. Have some variety in our lives to take the dullness out of life and add great memories and new meanings. Life is what we make it to be not what we think it should be. We have the resources and the power within us to create an atmosphere that's different from what we're familiar with. We all know that trying something different can trigger fear. This fear is triggered because we think a change may threaten our routine. However, the change will only help us to appreciate the routine in our lives that we sometimes take for granted.

October 20

Mind Opened by Wonderment

> "I would rather have a mind opened by won-
> der than one closed by belief."
> — Gerry Spence[255]

*W*hen we're in wonderment mode, we're
encouraging our imaginations to express
itself as it wishes to allow our minds to see
things that we haven't seen before. Wonderment helps us to break up limiting beliefs that
can keep us from making strives in our lives.
Wonderment is a good exercise to the mind because it helps to stimulate and expand our
minds beyond our beliefs system. The wonderment exercise also builds new associations,
which can help break up previous beliefs and
allow us to see that we have more choices in life.
Our minds don't have to be closed by our belief
but open by wonderment. We're curious crea-
tures because we want to know how things
work.

October 21

Light in the Heart

"Beauty is not in the face; beauty is a light in the heart." — Khalil[256]

Self-image is a conscious thing. How we interact with others is just a reflection of how we perceive ourselves. What we dislike about another person is really about the part we dislike about ourselves. And what we long for from others is really what we're not giving to others and ourselves. We will never find the one person who will fill the void of loneliness. We have to fill that void with a purposeful life. When we begin seeing the beauty in our hearts, then our appearance is no longer as important. Appearance is no longer important since we now know that we have others to care about us and we care for others because we looked beyond the faces, we see the light of beauty shining in their hearts as well as ours.

October 22

Hard Work Brings Also Luck

*"I am a great believer in luck. The harder I
work, the more of it I seem to have."*
— Coleman Cox[257]

*O*ur opportunities are greater when we work
diligently to meet our goals. That's why
we just have to hang in there during the time of
famine. With hard work and some bit of luck,
we will succeed. That's how we add to our good
luck is by working steadily towards our goal.
When the opportunity comes knocking at our
door, we will be ready to welcome it. Everything
is earned and what is given was merited somehow. So, the more we work on our goal, the
more opportunities there will be for the taking.
We just have to believe in ourselves for this to
happen and not allow our thoughts of self-doubt
to cripple us from the work that will pave the
way to success. We don't have to say to ourselves, "It is because of my background that I
shouldn't pursue my dreams." Instead, we
should pursue our dreams because of our background to bring a unique perspective on things.

October 23

The Mind in Rest

"True silence is the rest of the mind, and is to the spirit what sleep is to the body, nourishment and refreshment." — William Penn[258]

*E*xperiencing solitude helps our minds to clear up from our everyday busy lives. When we're in solitude by choice, it is easier to go within to experience our internal life. We have an internal life and external life. It is easier to get caught up in our external life that we don't have time to sit quietly alone. Our internal life is just as important as our external life. We need and have to respect both. If we can find a balance of both our internal and our external life, then we can lead a more productive life without experiencing burnout. Solitude is not loneliness. Loneliness is longing for the company of another while solitude is longing to get away from external stimuli. We all need to take a break from the fast pace of the world. If the mind is at rest, then the spirit and the body will follow.

October 24

Choose the Pain of Discipline

"Everyone must choose one of two pains: The pain of discipline or the pain of regret."
— Jim Rohn[259]

*I*n everyone's life, there is a pain of discipline and pain of regret. We all know from our own experiences that what we want will require from us is self-discipline. Discipline becomes painful when we would rather play. Discipline requires us to focus and concentrate on a task without being distracted on other external cues. Regrets make us look back on the promises we made for ourselves to do things but failed to keep. That's what makes regret feel so painful. Although the pain of discipline can intensify at the beginning, middle and ending, the pain of regret can last a lifetime. The wisdom that we all acquired through our experiences knows what to choose, and that is discipline.

October 25

Opportunities

> "Ability is of little account without
> opportunity."
> — Napoleon[260]

*I*t is good to be ready when an opportunity does approach us. We can always fine-tune our abilities until we find an opportunity to display them. Sometimes opportunities are contingent upon a need. Someone may need something done right away and would need the services of others. And sometimes we just have to pay closer attention to a problem that needs to be solved especially if it coincides with our abilities to help someone. Opportunities are there if we change the way we see things. There are opportunities that we have to wait for and there are other opportunities that we can create in one's life.

October 26

Start the Healing

"Our sorrows and wounds are healed only
when we touch them with compassion."
— Buddha[261]

Sometimes we keep our pain because we want to keep the person or the event in our lives that caused the initial pain. Therefore, we can't move forward in our lives. If the person(s) or the event(s) that caused the initial pain is no longer in our lives, we gravitate to another person or reenact the event. This isn't compassion since we can't heal our sorrows and wounds. It is time to say goodbye to our sorrows and wounds. We no longer have to be defined by them because those things happened in our past. We're only hurting ourselves no longer the person in our past. Once we realize that it is ourselves that are causing the hurt, we then can stop them and start healing by forgiving the past individual(s) and then ourselves for continuing the pain by letting go. This is compassion.

October 27

Birth and Death

"I had seen birth and death but had thought they were different." — T. S. Eliot[262]

While death is an exit from this world, birth is access to this world. We live our lives between two unknowns, birth and death. We have no memory of our birth and death. Just like sleep, we won't know that we're dead until we awaken from it. Our physical bodies return to the mother earth while the mother's body takes nutrients from the soil to give to the unborn to grow. Before birth, there was darkness and then light, and at the time of death, there was darkness and then light. During the gestation period, the mother takes care of her body for the preparation of a new life to be born, and most of us, either through sickness or hospice care, are preparing ourselves for the inevitable death. Is birth the beginning or the ending, and is death the ending or the beginning?

October 28

Heavy Burden to Carry

"I ask not for a lighter burden, but for broader shoulders." — Jewish Proverb[263]

*W*e do want to have a lighter burden but that's not always possible if we want to make a difference in our progress. Instead of looking for a short cut, why not grow into the role we want so that we can make a difference in our lives. We get broader shoulders when we struggle through life's challenges. We all have burdens to carry, but there are unnecessary burdens we carry. We've just got to look for those unnecessary burdens and stop carrying them because they only hold us back with not much energy left. Broader shoulders can only carry so much for so long in one's life. Once we let go of those unnecessary burdens, we're more than able to handle most anything with broader shoulders.

October 29

It's in the Struggles

> "Changes and progress very rarely are gifts from above. They come out of struggles from below." — Noam Chomsky[264]

$\mathcal{N}$ow we are at the speed at which our learnings have slowed down since we've been adults. We've experienced being stuck because we've become set in our ways. But now we have a desire to want to change and don't know how. And we find ourselves forgetting that we do have a storehouse of resources that we can tap into to help to make a change so that we can fulfill our wants or our desires in our lives. The treasure is the resource of experiences that every one of us possesses. We just have to be reminded of our struggles to learn how to walk by taking our first steps, or our struggles to learn how to read our first book, or our struggles to learn how to ride our first bike, or our struggles to learn how to do anything new for the first time. This is good news because we can look back to see in our past that we have gone through each struggle in which we can build upon and we can make today's struggles easier to handle. This is our newfound mind-set.

October 30

What Can We Learn From?

"If you find a path with no obstacles, it probably doesn't lead anywhere."
— Frank A. Clark[265]

*W*e shouldn't see obstacles as our nemesis but rather as a way to measure ourselves. Obstacles can tell us how we're growing in our journey. We have all experienced obstacles in our unique way. Obstacles aren't meant for us to fail but are meant for us to grow into what we want to be in our lives. Obstacles chip away the edges of our biases as long as we have a stick-to-it-ness attitude. It is easy to have the attitude in the classic Aesop's Fables of the fox who couldn't reach the grapes and only to give up by saying that those grapes were sour anyway. Instead, we can have the attitude that we can learn something about ourselves about how we deal with obstacles, and about how we dealt with obstacles in the past. Our pasts are our resources of experiences up to now that we can use to fulfill our dreams and desires.

October 31

Valuing Our Talents

> "Too many people overvalue what they are not
> and undervalue what they are."
> — Malcolm S. Forbes[266]

*W*e overvalue what we are not when our egos are inflated. We don't want to settle for what we already have. Therefore, we don't use our talents or appreciate our talents enough. Each one of us is given talents so that we can use them for a purposeful way. If we need an ego boost, then purposefully using our talent can be satisfying and it will be an ego boost. Life brings meaning into our lives when we purposefully use our talents.

November 1

On Becoming a Habit

"The hard must become habit. The habit must become easy. The easy must become beautiful." — Doug Henning[267]

It is easy to find us admiring another person's talent in how he or she uses what seems to be without effort. We forget that it took that person's time and dedication to acquire such a high level of skill. We think learning a skill is all physical work, however, the brain is involved also while developing new neural pathways. It is a mind and body learning experience. The brain is learning how to coordinate the unfamiliar arm movements all the while sending signals or communication back and forth. Just about everything we learn at first will take some effort to develop adequately and then beautifully at the end. And that's how habits are made, whether they're good or bad. We use our habits to our advantage when we need them to work for us.

November 2

Big Dreams and Small Fears

"Miracles start to happen when you give as much energy to your dreams as you do to your fears." — Richard Wilkins[268]

*F*ears can interfere with our dreams. Our dreams become smaller when we spend so much energy on self-doubt. Dreams are our hopes for what we wish to do or become in the future. Dreams help us to imagine ourselves in the future doing what we've been wanting to do. If we can redirect the energy of our fears toward our dreams, then we can see before our eyes how a dream becomes something that we can now touch. Milton H. Erickson once said that there is little to fear. Our fears have a way not only to control us but to control others as well. Fear won't allow us to imagine the possibility of an alternative because imagination helps us to open up our minds for understandings, thus decreasing our anxiety.

November 3

Reflection of Our Experiences

> "If it's still in your mind, it is worth taking the risk." — Paulo Coelho[269]

We all can imagine something we want to make real in our lives. Imagination is very powerful because we can rehearse as many ways possible in our minds for how we want something to be. Imagination allows us to recreate things in our minds without judgment. Imagination allows us to take risks first in our minds before we risk making the idea real. Imagination is a gift that everyone has who is human. Imagination is a reflection of our experiences. It is the visual memory, spatial skills, motor skills, and other senses that we have re-experienced in our imagination and our dreams.

November 4

What I Choose to Become

"I am not what happened to me, I am what I choose to become."— Carl Jung[270]

*W*e don't have to be victims of what we can't control. Instead, we can choose to be the victor of what we can control. It can be easy to fall into a trap of always lamenting about the unpleasant events in one's life. It is not easy to pull one's self out of such a trap, but the good news is that is not impossible. It is not impossible to find another way or find an alternative or to adopt a new perspective. Thinking differently is the key to becoming a victor.

November 5

Accepting Our Weaknesses

> "Growth begins when we begin to accept our weaknesses."— Jean Vanier[271]

Accepting our weaknesses means that we're first admitting to ourselves that we have imperfections or limitations. For us to grow, we must confront the reality that we have limitations. We don't have to always yield to them but we can work around them. They don't have to directly affect our lives negatively. We can use them to our advantage so we may be role models to others having a hard time accepting their weaknesses. Growing is having the understanding that we can find other ways to better ourselves without finding a reason to not push ourselves. It is very easy to find a reason not to improve our situation when we're only looking at our weaknesses and not looking at the possibility of growth. If we see possibilities in ourselves, then our blinds are open to see opportunities.

November 6

Look at Both Sides

"Stop being afraid of what could go wrong,
and focus on what could go right."
— Unknown[272]

*W*hen we anticipate what could go wrong,
it is our clue to ourselves that we're
afraid to put ourselves out there. We're afraid to
be and feel vulnerable because this creates discomfort. It is all right to see what could go
wrong, but it is also all right to see what could
go right. It would be good to our advantage to
see both sides and not only be looking at only
positive or only the negative side of things.
When we look at what could go wrong, we can
come up with a plan and be prepared to deal
with it just as we can create a plan to build on
what could go right in the situation.

November 7

Cherish Today

"Before someone's tomorrow has been taken away, cherish those you love, appreciate them today." — Michelle C. Ustaszeski[273]

*W*e don't know how long we have on this earth. Instead of wishing that we spent more quality time with our friends and family, today is our opportunity to make that phone call or visit those we cherish and appreciate. We can be thankful that we still have a family while others especially during the holidays have no family with which to spend time. Family brings support, closeness, and connectedness that we all need. We want to feel belonged and not be alone. We need each other because we're a community of people. Tomorrow is not guaranteed, but certainly, we have today.

November 8

Completion Is Better

"**What is not started today is never finished tomorrow.**"— Johann Wolfgang von Goethe[274]

*N*ow is the most important time to start. Thinking about it is very different from starting it. When starting something, it is our goal to finish it sometime in the future. Some of us have many start-up projects to only become unfinished projects. Although it takes courage to start something new, it also takes determination to finish it. If we break big projects into smaller ones, then we don't have to feel overwhelmed or burdened by the vast size of the project. It is possible to finish a project as long as we start with small pieces. Finishing a piece at a time reinforces our confidence in completing all the pieces.

November 9

Tomorrow's Dream

"Don't let today's disappointments cast a shadow on tomorrow's dreams."— Unknown[275]

*T*oday will be in the past tomorrow. We can look at our disappointments as a learning experience. We can find a positive side if we look for one. We don't have to be influenced by yesterday's disappointments. A good question we can ask ourselves is why was our response a disappointment? The disappointments were based on a certain expectation we had on an event. For example, we probably wanted to get something to accomplish that day, or we didn't come up with an idea on a project. As long as we make an effort and don't give in, in due time, things will turn around. Our unconscious mind continues to search for ideas way long after we call it a day. Our unconscious mind is always preparing us for the next day.

November 10

Making Our Days Better

"I cannot make my days longer so I strive to make them better."— Henry David Thoreau[276]

*O*ne of the hallmarks of procrastinating is when we tried to make our days longer. We tried to fool ourselves into believing that we have more time to do something so we continue to delay until we feel the pressure of a deadline to start a project. We don't have to spend most of our time doing nothing but thinking about how much time we have left to do something. We can instead plan where we want our time to be spent on what projects. It is really up to us because we're in charge of whatever we do in life. We can make our days a little better each time we initiate.

November 11

The Creative Way

*C*reativity is our way to freedom. Creativity can widen the scope of our minds. Most people who are successful are also very creative. Creative people are willing to open up their minds when they don't know and want to learn. Creative people see things that others can't see or imagined. It takes courage to let go of old patterns to develop new patterns. Old patterns are really old beliefs that are out-of-date. Just like computer software; if we want our computers to run smoothly, then we must routinely update the software. We need to routinely update our belief system for us to continue to adapt and interact with the world around us.

November 12

A New Beginning

*"Nobody can go back and start a new begin-
ning, but anyone can start today and make a
new ending."*— Maria Robinson[277]

*I*t is too late to go back to our past to start
over. There is nothing we can do to
change our past. However, we can learn from
our past. We can learn about what we've done
wrong, and what we've done right in our past.
Our past can be our guide to what we're going
to do today. We know that certain things we do
will lead us to nowhere because we've gone
through this before. Today is our opportunity to
start a new chapter in our lives. Every day is an
opportunity to do what is right for us. What we
do today is based on what we did yesterday.
We've made certain decisions, which affect us
today whether the decisions were positive or
negative. If we want to be at a certain place in
the future, then today is the day we got to make
decisions, or if we had already made decisions,
then we ought to follow up on them to make
sure that we're still on the right track.

November 13

Reminiscing

I t is nice to reunite with old friends that we haven't seen in a while. There is something about reuniting with friends that recharges us. There is something about reminiscing the past; it feels as though it was just yesterday and not twenty years ago. We recall the good times in our lives. While we look back, we can laugh at ourselves and with each other. There is no need to regret past times. Our perspective is different when we recall old memories. We realize that we don't have to take life so seriously instead to seriously live life as we so desire, with friends.

November 14

In Suffering Is Blessings

"Never to suffer would never to have been blessed."— Edgar Allen Poe[278]

*W*hether or not that's emotional or physical suffering, we can still say that we're blessed. To be blessed is to look for all the wonderful things that happened in one's life while suffering. The things that we cherish in our hearts the most are the things that are blessings to us. Suffering is only temporary and that's a blessing to know. Nothing is permanent, and that includes suffering. Suffering is our resistance to pain. However, it is a natural propensity to withdraw our hand from a hot burning stove because getting burnt and feeling the pain is inevitable. It's self-preservation to withdraw one's hand. But we can start counting our blessings with our fingers. This is by far the best way to put our hands to good use.

November 15

Golden Idea

*G*ood ideas are like gold. They are rare finds. Ideas tend to pop into our heads when we least expect them. An idea doesn't come our way easily when we're forced to think up one. If an idea comes up by forced thinking, that ideas tends to be counter-intuitive, and may seem to be wacky. But ideas that come without force are the ones that seem to stimulate our minds more into wanting to explore and to expand them. It just takes one idea to move a mountain, to alter thought, and to change the world. Ideas stimulate our imagination. Good ideas light up the mind like a Christmas tree; they're nice to look at.

November 16

Kindness, No Matter How Small

> "No act of kindness, no matter how small, is
> ever wasted."— Aesop[279]

$\mathcal{W}$e need kindness when we feel most embarrassed. Every ounce of kindness is used when we're lost. A touch of kindness makes our whole day. Kindness builds self-respect. Kindness brings us together as one. Kindness balances everything. Kindness can melt away anger when it's appropriate. Kindness illuminates the entire room. Kindness helps us to put faith back into humanity. Kindness brings out the good in people. We can never be too kind when kindness is needed. We may forget a name, but we will never forget a kind person. Giving away kindness is just as good as receiving it.

November 17

Give and Live

> "We make a living by what we get, but we make a life by what we give."
> — Winston Churchill[280]

*L*iving life is about giving ourselves to the service of humanity and our environment. What we've learned through our past experiences and what others have taught us can be passed on to others who are willing to learn to make their lives better. Giving is a selfless act. We give not because we want to feel good but because we want to do what's right. Giving helps us to connect with others. Giving is a blessing for the giver as well as for the receiver of the gift. Giving is nature's ways of keeping things in balance. Just as a mother gives herself selflessly to her child, so that child, as an adult, gives himself selflessly to his children. And so on.

November 18

We Are Here to Live

*W*e don't stop growing or learning when we accomplish something. Life is not over when we accomplish something. Our accomplishments are just the icing on the cake of our experiences. We are here to live life. Life is not necessarily about getting the grand prize at the end, but about living. Each time we accomplish our goal, we gain confidence in ourselves to continue what makes us happy in life. Our accomplishments reinforce the need to express our idea into something we can teach others. So we don't have to lose sight of what is important in life. Learning, living, and experiencing each day is all we need to express our life's satisfaction.

November 19

Tap Your Potential

*E*very one of us has potential that we haven't tapped into yet. We have potential that we didn't know we had. It is never too late to find out about one's self. Although we know a lot about ourselves, we can still discover more things about ourselves. Our strength comes from our latent potentials because we took the courage to access them. We don't have to be afraid to embrace our potentials and find out what we're made of.

November 20

Don't Give Up

"The strongest people aren't always the people who win, but the people who don't give up when they lose."— Ashley Hodgeson[281]

*W*e don't have to always need to win something for us to experience achievement. Achievement is acquired through a series of losses. Losses that we can learn to get stronger each time we attempt something in our lives. Losing is not the ending of a project, but the beginning of gaining wisdom from the experience of losses. There will be a lot of losses before we begin to see our battles won.

November 21

When Time Stops

> "Even if I knew that tomorrow the world would go to pieces, I would still plant my apple tree." — Martin Luther[282]

*O*rienting towards the future is about sowing seeds today because we don't know what the future will bring. But today is a sure thing to do to alter our future to what we want it to be. It is also about living today, and if we get another day to live, we can continue to bring about an even better future. It would be like a nice bite of an apple from the tree that we had planted some time earlier. We can be thankful when that time comes because it helps us to understand that something we did in our past had some control over what's happening today in our lives. Time is so precious and can be easily wasted if we don't use it to our advantage. When time is lost, we can never get it back. However, we must go on living because everything else will.

November 22

When Feeling Stuck

*W*hen we're feeling stuck, it means that we haven't made a change yet. When we're feeling stuck, it means we haven't done anything yet. When we're feeling stuck, it means we haven't made up our minds yet. When we're feeling stuck, it means we aren't growing. When we're feeling stuck, it means we're doing the same things we have done before expecting a different outcome. When we're feeling stuck, it means that we're waiting for something to happen. When we're feeling stuck, it means that we're looking in the wrong direction and it also means that we haven't taken charge of our lives. We need to take charge of our lives and feel like we have more control over our lives. We don't have to wait on anyone or anything to start taking charge of our lives; therefore, we no longer have to feel stuck.

November 23

See the Positive Side

"See the positive side, the potential, and make an effort."— Dalai Lama[283]

There is a positive side to every negative side. If we're always looking at the negative side of things, then we squeeze out the positive side of things. If we want to be fair about it we should look at the negative and the positive side of things equally. As Dalai Lama suggests in the quote that if we see the positive side of things, then we will see the potentials or opportunities we can take, and then we might want to make the effort to bring things into reality or to change things.

November 24

Cheerfulness

**"Cheerfulness is the best promoter of
health."— Proverb**[284]

*W*hen we see someone in a cheerful mood,
we want to know, what is it that makes
him or her so cheerful? We all have experienced
feeling good after being around a cheerful person. It makes us feel good for the rest of the day.
We feel more alive when we're in a cheerful
mood and that everything seems okay again.
Being cheerful makes a difference in health and
well-being. Yes, we're all responsible for taking
care of our health, and this is just as important
as taking care of our mental health.

November 25

When an Idea Is Fully Ripe

$\int$ ometimes, we wish an idea could come to our minds quickly, but that's not the way things always happen. We have to wait for an idea to fully ripen in the background of our minds before it is released to the foreground of our minds. When an idea is released to the foreground of our mind we should take notice. If we don't take notice, then the idea will vaporize into nothingness. An idea has a short life span. If we look for ideas, then they will make themselves available. Ideas will only grow if we take hold of them and nourish them into something that alters or expand our minds.

November 26

Holiday of Thanks

*I*f we break down the word "Thanksgiving", we get "thanks" and "giving." Let's focus on the first part. When someone gives us his or her time and effort, after it is finished we politely say "thank you" and with a reply "you're welcome." This is a ritual that we use because it is polite and that we value and appreciate the time that the other person gives. We know it takes the effort to give to another and when someone is thankful for the services we put forth; it is very much appreciated to know that we made another person happy. Respect is given by both parties through this transaction and this mutual experience encourages more of the same.

November 27

Don't Let Doubting Ideas
Get in Our Way

Sometimes we allow limited ideas to get in our way. It is easy to have a perfect vision of ourselves doing something we would like to do, but we forget that for us to get close to that image in our minds, we need to start working on it now because it takes work and time for us to get there. If we want it, then we must obtain it by great labor. Great labor means that we have to make certain sacrifices. For example, some sacrifices we could make might be staying up late to study or getting up at 5:00 am to exercise for a marathon. When we begin to think of the amount of work that we have to do to match the image in our minds, we begin to doubt that it can't be done. Doubt sets in this way before we start. Instead, we can test the doubting ideas by actually starting the process. We will notice that yes, it is difficult, however, we don't mind doing it, because we begin to realize that we are making it happen. We are moving forward and toward our goals.

November 28

New Behaviors and New Thinking

*F*or us to change a behavior we have to replace it with another behavior. We developed behaviors to meet a certain need, but when that need is met, we no longer need the behavior. The behavior is obsolete. It is difficult to let go of the behavior because it is so ingrained in our psyche. The behavior becomes a part of our personality. It is time to replace the behavior with a new one when the behavior becomes a problem instead of a solution. This is done gradually and slowly with a lot of patience. The old behaviors usually are attached to an old pattern of thinking. Replacing an old behavior with a new one will break up the old pattern of thinking into something fresh and new.

November 29

Dignity

*D*ignity is about how we see our worthiness. No matter how we fall, we can get up with dignity. Dignity is having self-worth. Self-worth is about believing in self. Dignity is about being in equal footing with another. Dignity is about treating ourselves with respect while treating others with respect. Dignity is not about what we can get out of something but how can we contribute or how can we serve others. Dignity says that we are just as important as the next person. Dignity is having self-esteem. We can see things in ourselves that are good as well as in others.

November 30

Laughter Is One Way

"He who laughs at himself never runs out of
things to laugh at." — Epictetus[285]

*I*t is all right to not take things so seriously all the time. It is all right to laugh at ourselves. When we laugh at our foibles, we are more accepting, we like ourselves, and we free ourselves from ourselves. Freedom is the recognition that we can allow ourselves to be and feel like ourselves—in other words, we can feel comfortable in our skin. We all have experienced uncertainty, vulnerability, and exposure. These things make us uneasy. However, it is good to experience these things in our lives so we know what we're about. It is about how we deal with uncertainty, vulnerability, and exposure that's important. And laughter is one way of dealing.

December 1

Our Life Is Like a Canvas

*O*ur life is like a canvas. We can live as freely as we wish. If we want to draw a sun and then paint it green, we can. If we want to draw water and then paint it goldenrod, we can. However we want to paint our canvases, we can do that. Just as we can paint our canvases, we can express freely how we want to live our lives. Sometimes we find ourselves painting our canvases black and white, or gray because we're experiencing a feeling of being stuck. But to get unstuck, we need to start using our paintbrush and brush in some color to bring out our vibrant picture of life.

December 2

Inspiration Moves Us

*I*nspiration is the feeling we get when something touches our souls. Inspiration moves us to do something worthwhile. How come we're touched by inspiration? Inspirations reawaken us to think of the possibility to do something that's beyond ourselves. Others inspire us by their example. Someone's creativity inspires us to do better in our own craft. Someone's body of work creates inspiration for their admirers. It is something inside us that draws us collectively to inspiration. Inspiration is like food to the soul. Inspiration helps us to know that we can do great things in our lives as well. Inspiration can make us believe that nothing is impossible. Inspiration helps us to align and connect to our mind, body, and soul.

December 3

Life's Problems

> "Life's problems wouldn't be called hurdles if
> there wasn't a way to get over them."
> — Unknown[286]

*T*he above quote uses a metaphor to describe problems as hurdles. Hurdles are meant to jump over from the start and until the finish line. From the day we're born and until the day we die, we will always be dealing with problems. Just as an athlete who jumps one hurdle at a time, we have to work on one problem at a time. Sometimes problems can't be solved, but other times they resolve themselves.

December 4

A Little Pressure

$\mathcal{O}$ nly if we make our problems smaller, then maybe we can deal with them better. It's all right to feel a little pressure when we're faced with a challenge to complete a task. A little pressure can be motivating especially when there is a deadline we have to meet. It is better to set deadlines for ourselves because if we don't, then nothing will get done. We don't have to look at deadlines as punishment but as encouragement. When we set deadlines, we are forced to use our time most effectively instead of procrastinating and waiting for the last minutes to do it. Waiting for the last minutes is just putting unnecessary pressure on us while trying to complete 85 percent of the work in a short amount of time. Some of us thrive on this kind of pressure and like it. However, the anticipation of wondering whether or not to start today or tomorrow can be agonizing.

December 5

What Do We Know Is Certain?

*W*hat we know is certain is that we're alive. What we know is certain is that we get hungry and/or thirsty. What we know is certain is that we want to know about life. What we know is certain is that there are a lot of uncertainties. What we know is certain is that change is constant. What we know is certain is that we experience pain. What we know is certain is that we experience joy. What we know is certain is that we're born, we live, then we die. What we know is certain is that it rains and snows, and the wind blows, and the sun shines.

December 6

When There Is Difficulty, There Is Growth

*W*hen we are having a hard time, it's an opportunity for growth. When life seems unfair, it is an opportunity to comfort others. When we fall down, it is an opportunity to get up and even help others up. When it rains and thunders, it is an opportunity to look for rainbows. When it gets dark, it is an opportunity to see the stars. When we see disaster, it is an opportunity to give in some way. When we get tired, it is an opportunity to rest. When we don't understand, it is an opportunity to learn. When things are chaotic, it is an opportunity to seek peace from within.

December 7

What's Stopping You?

*W*hatever we are doing or not doing is all based on a belief system. It is no coincidences that our actions are based on a belief system that we use every day. We no longer think about what we need to do next because most of our actions are done unconsciously. But when we first learn something new our actions are made consciously and deliberately. We may now wonder why we struggle to obtain our goals or procrastinate at the last minute to start doing what we set out to do a couple of months earlier. In other words, what is stopping us from obtaining our goals? What are the beliefs that we're saying to ourselves are somehow stopping us from doing what we want for our lives? These are questions that we can ask ourselves.

December 8

Light a Lamp

"If you light a lamp for someone else, it will also brighten your path." — Buddha[287]

We help ourselves when we help others in need. It is better to give back than to receive. But to be most effective in assisting others in need, we first have to make sure that our needs are being met. We also need ourselves renewed and with supply reserves before we can give to others. Time is well spent when we show compassion for others through our sacrifice. Compassion is good for those who are giving it and good for those who are receiving it. Compassion is like turning on a lamp to brighten up a room.

December 9

Enjoying This Point in Time

> "The whole life of a man is but a point in time;
> let us enjoy it." — Plutarch[288]

*W*e get so busy with the tasks that we forget to enjoy the hard work we put into it. It's all right to allow ourselves to enjoy our lives since we have only one life. Our whole life is maybe a speck but it doesn't mean that we are insignificant. All that matters is how significant we see our lives, because it is ours to live. We are born, we live and then we die. We are born into this life and death will take us out of this life. Since the former already has happened, then let us enjoy our time alive and together until the latter comes. Yesterday is gone forever and tomorrow has yet to arrive, but today is here, a moment to enjoy.

December 10

When It Is Time

*W*hen it is time to rest, then let us rest. When it is time to work, then let us work. When it is time to eat, then let us enjoy eating, with family. When it is time to meet up with others, then let us meet up. Everything has a place and time as long as we are there doing them. When it is time to rise, then let us rise. We are all interconnected with the universe. Although we are part of a bigger picture, we each do our parts as contributors to the society we live in. No one is insignificant because every one of us is unique. There will never be another one like us. So, let us roam freely being ourselves because it is the natural thing to do. Why should we resist what's natural? As humans, we live at a higher order of things and we are stewards of this world. We're here only temporarily until the next generations come along to be the new leaders of their time.

December 11

Life's Like a Movie

"Life's like a movie, write your own ending.
Keep believing, keep pretending."
— Jim Henson[289]

*W*e can write our script. We don't have to follow some else's path. Instead, we are here to figure out our way. We each have a unique set of circumstances that we can draw from that will help determine our path. We keep believing in ourselves to continue to move forward to where we want to go in life. We keep pretending so that sooner or later we become what we've dreamed of doing. We each have to walk our path for us to grow into what we want to become. What we become is what determines how we will write our ending.

December 12

A Game of Cards

"Life is like a game of cards. The hand you are dealt is determinism; the way you play it is free will." — Jawaharlal Nehru[290]

*W*e all come from unique circumstances, which means we have a unique perspective on things. We each have to struggle with the cards that are dealt with us every day of our lives but are unique to us. Our fate doesn't have to be determined by circumstances. Not everyone was born with a fortune; not everyone had a perfect upbringing. But we do have a free will to overcome our unique circumstances somehow. When things are difficult, it is easy to say that we can't do it because of our background. We ought not to give up or make excuses to stop. Yes, we have free will, however, using our free will is an opportunity for us to rise above circumstances and to live our lives as we see fit with integrity.

December 13

Waiting for the Right Moment

*T*here is a time to wait and there is a time to move. It's all right to wait for the right moment to act, especially when we want our movements to be impactful. There is a time to wait for the right moment to speak and there is a time to do a lot of listening. Timing is just as important as spontaneity. There is a time and a place for both depending on the circumstances. What we say is just as important as how we say it. When we were infants, we began by learning how to recognize different adult facial expressions. We learned the meanings behind the facial expressions just as we learned how to understand the meaning behind vocal sounds.

December 14

Making Decisions

*W*e ought not to allow circumstances to dictate our life. Instead, we ought to make decisions based on how we want to live our lives. Let us not wait for something to happen that may force our hand to make choices that we are not ready for. And let us not delay but start doing something now to make progress. Time is of the essence. Better to start now instead of waiting for something to happen later. It is easier to talk about what we want to do than to actually do it. Starting something new can be the hardest thing to do first but after that, it gets easier. We just have to remember that there is always a learning curve to everything we do, we've just got to be patient with ourselves.

December 15

Blessings and Lessons

"Some people come into your life as blessings. Others come into your life as lessons."
— Mother Teresa[291]

We learn a lot about ourselves when we're dealing with a difficult person. We learn how angry we can get. We learn what we dislike about that person. We want to change them to the way we think they should behave. Some of the things we have difficulty with about that person are just a reflection of what we dislike about ourselves. It's the parts we hate that we reflect on others. We all have foibles that we have to accept about ourselves. So we begin looking at the things we do like about ourselves and start looking for those positive things or traits in others. That way we can see the whole person instead of just singling out negative traits.

December 16

Lost Time

> "Lost time is never found again."
> — Benjamin Franklin[292]

*W*e all know that it is better to use our time wisely than to waste it. We don't know how valuable time is until we're faced with a deadline or an external consequence. We're motivated to complete a task when the time is about to run out instead of using the time we had before. We will never get back the time we had before. The only thing we can do is to make time. We make time by looking at what are the available times we have to complete our task. When we schedule our time into something, we're defining the amount of time to get a specific goal achieved or specific task completed. The time we truly have is now. So it's going to takes some thinking on how best to use our time.

December 17

When Children Look for Magic

*C*hildren look for magic because it stimulates curiosity. Children want to learn how the magic is done. There is a lot of magic in the world; magic is a thing that is unexplained. When we see magic, we only see what the magician wants us to see. It's like watching our imagination come to life before our eyes. As adults when we see a trick done, we're in conflict with ourselves because we know there is an explanation to the trick but at the same time, we don't want to know. We want to keep the experience of trick that the magician performed as a mystery.

December 18

Stop Trying to Be Normal, Be Amazing

"If you are always trying to be normal, you will never know how amazing you can be."
— Maya Angelou[293]

We want to be normal because we want to fit in. However, we don't have to be ostracized by a group of our peers. If we think that we will be ostracized by our peers, then our peers also fear to be different. How can we find out how amazing we can be if we are afraid to really be ourselves? We don't have to hide all our foibles; we've just got to accept them so we don't have to fear rejection from others. Every day we have the opportunity to know how amazing we can be if we accept everything about us.

December 19

Create Your Own Atmosphere

*W*e don't have to wait until a change of atmosphere; instead, we can create our own atmosphere. It's like moving into a new office. If we want our office to feel welcoming, then we can put up a picture of positive messages or use bright colors to help create a positive atmosphere.

Every holiday is an opportunity to celebrate with decorations. Each holiday has a theme. We can do the same in our personal life create a new theme if we're dissatisfied. When we create another theme, we are changing the atmosphere. Just simply cleaning the house or doing yard work can create a welcoming atmosphere.

December 20

Slow and Steady

*W*hen we rush things, it is inevitable that we are going to miss something, forget something and make unnecessary mistakes. But if we take our time in the beginning, we will notice things ahead of time and won't easily forget and only make fewer mistakes. When we pace ourselves, we are developing a rhythm from within. Pacing ourselves helps us to stay balanced and not get overly stressed. Pacing ourselves also helps us to complete things. The rhythm we create within us rewards us with the satisfaction we get from our efforts.

December 21

Breaking Free from Beliefs and Judgements

"Taking responsibility for your beliefs and judgments gives you the power to change them."— Byron Katie[294]

*I*f we claim ownership of our beliefs and judgments, then we have the opportunity and the power to change them. We don't have to feel powerless anymore when the opportunity to change is there. We just have to be willing to learn to enlarge our way of thinking. This doesn't mean we have to compromise what matters to us. Our goal is to break free of our minds to see beyond our beliefs and judgments. When our minds become free then we can be open to new ideas. New ideas create new associations and new understandings for us.

December 22

Meaning Breathes Life

"Love is just a word until someone comes along and gives it meaning."— Unknown[295]

*H*ow can we reach an understanding about things, if we don't give it meaning? It is like listening to a new song for the first time. We can't relate to the new song until we begin to build associations around it. After building new associations with the song, it becomes meaningful to us. We begin to link current events in our lives to the new song. The song becomes real to us. That's why we enjoy listening to old songs we grew up with because they trigger past memories, images, and feelings. We re-experience past events as though they were yesterday. The songs from past events are now more meaningful than before because they take us back to a place we have forgotten about so long ago. It is like watching a black and white picture slowly changing to various colors.

December 23

In the End

"It is good to have an end to journey toward; but it is the journey that matters, in the end."
— Ursula K. Le Guin[296]

In the end, we will look back on our journey. There is a beginning, a middle, and an ending of our lives. At the beginning our path was unclear, in the middle our path became clearer, and in the end, we see the entirety of our life. During our reflection, we will see things we did that surprise us. We see the different times in our lives we displayed unbelievable courage through our ups and downs. We've struggled through life when it seemed there was no end in sight. We laughed, and we cried in our frustrations. We experienced the cycle of life and what it meant to us. We wander aimlessly at times and then bootstrapped ourselves back on track. For the most part, we did our best, but a few times we failed—though we picked ourselves back up and started walking again.

December 24

First Be Gentle

> "Be gentle first with yourself if you wish to be gentle with others."— Lama Yeshe[297]

*W*e ought to allow room for us to make mistakes and gently correct them. Self-criticism is just another form of self-blame. Blaming doesn't support growth. So, it is better to encourage growth than to look for mistakes. Mistakes are inevitable because we're humans. Mistakes only reveal new self-discoveries. Discoveries will help us understand one another without passing judgment. Being gentle goes further than being coerced into something we're not ready for. Knowing self is also about understanding others. We all have dreams, we all have concerns, and we have more similarity than dissimilarity.

December 25

We Are the Pilot of Our Time

> "The bad news is time flies. The good news is you're the pilot."— Michael Altshuler[298]

*W*e have control over what we do with our time. While we wait somewhere in a long line, we can think about our next plan, or fill our time with reading a book, chatting with someone. The time we have now allows us to do what we want to do. Time is valuable. Time allows us to see things from a different perspective. Everything has a deadline. We all have unfinished things that we want to go back to, if we use our time wisely, we can finish them. Time helps us to prioritize what's most important to us. Time ticks, ticks, and ticks away.

December 26

Touch Them with Compassion

> "Our sorrows and wounds are healed only
> when we touch them with compassion."
> —Buddha[299]

We have all experienced sorrows and wounds sometimes in our lives. Sometimes in our lives, we have all experienced being touched with compassion while we're in the midst of sorrows. Human contact is so important when we're feeling like we're experiencing sorrows and pain alone. Compassion from others is the stronghold that will help get us through some of the most difficult times in our lives. We just have to allow others in our world to share their compassion for us. So, the next time, we will be more understandable and feel empathy and give compassion to others who are hurting and in sorrow.

December 27

Having the Courage

I t is true that what we have imagined is what will become real in our world. If we imagine the worst, then we will find and look for something that will make it the worst. If we imagine optimism in a difficult situation, then in our minds we will see a better outcome. It is really about how we see it in our minds. That's how powerful the brain or the mind, is. If we focus on one thing to complete, we will find a way to get to the end. But if we allow ourselves to get distracted, then we will be definitely be distracted. It's not necessarily about whether we're able to do something; rather, it's about having the courage to do it.

December 28

Building Confidence

*I*t is through confidence we do our best work. We begin to realize that we can do what we doubted earlier in the process. Each time we attempt on something, we improve on it. Persistence begets improvement while improvement leads to excelling in our work. The more our confidence grows the more we have self-reliance and the wisdom to know to let go of the things we can't do. But we can lend those things to someone else who has that special talent.

December 29

The Joy in Looking

"Joy in looking and comprehending is nature's most beautiful gift."— **Albert Einstein**[300]

*I*f we want to learn sometime outside ourselves, observe things around us. Sometimes, for us to understand ourselves, we have to look beyond ourselves. The world teaches us things about others and about ourselves and that's a beautiful gift. We are here to learn and to experience life as we live it and to explore our curiosity about things, things that can enrich our lives, and to share with one another. Things we share bring us together and that's what counts— is each other.

December 30

A Day for a Life

**"What you do today is important, because you
are exchanging a day of your life for it."
— Unknown[301]**

*W*hen we look at the above quotes that
way, we begin to see how important it is
to prioritize our lives. What we value the most is
what we should spend our lives doing, because
we would exchange the days of our lives for it.
Every moment counts because we are spending
our lives living in that moment. As we pause
and reflect on our lives at this moment, we see
that it's okay to clear up what's weighing on our
minds. Those things that are weighing on our
minds vanish when we stop for a moment to
reflect on what is important.

December 31

We Have 365 Days Left

*H*ow come we think we need a resolution at the beginning of the year to make a change? Because is easier to say to ourselves we have 365 days to do this or that. For some of us who procrastinate, we fool ourselves into thinking that we have 365 days left to start something new. Instead, we ought to make a deadline each day or to do a list each day and follow it until most things are completed. It is all right to add one new thing to a list to do so we can have variety. If we're going to try something new, we need to commit to it for a certain period so we know what we're getting ourselves into. Remember, always at the beginning of doing something new, not only starting but also maintaining it will be difficult at first. We just have to be patient with ourselves and not give up.

References

1. Unknown Author. https://tinybuddha.
    com/wisdom-quotes/open-minds-lead-
    to-open-doors/ Retrieved 06/02/2020.
2. Thomas A. Edison, https://
    www.brainyquote.com/quotes/
    thomas_a_edison_149061 Retrieved
    06/07/2020.
3. Chico Xavier. https://www.goodreads.
    com/quotes/375516-though-nobody-
    can-go-back-and-make-a-new-begin
    ning?page=5. Retrieved 6/07/2020.
4. Jonatan Martensson. https://tinybud
    dha.com/wisdom-quotes/success-will-
    never-be-a-big-step-in-the-future-suc
    cess-is-a-small-step-taken-just-now/
    Retrieved 6/07/2020.
5. Zig Ziglar. http://www.changeforhealth.
    com/communication-and-understanding/
    Retrieve 6/07/2020.
6. H. Jackson Brown, Jr. https://
    www.brainyquote.com/quotes/h_jack
    son_brown_jr_382774.
    Retrieve 06/07/2020.
7. John Rohn. https://www.goodreads.com/
    quotes/341435-either-you-run-the-day-
    or-the-day-runs-you.
    Retrieve 6/07/2020.

References

8. Unknown. https://tinybuddha.com/wis
    dom-quotes/a-truly-happy-person-is-
    one-who-can-enjoy-the-scenery-while-
    on-a-detour/ Retrieved 6/09/2020.
9. Unknown. https://tinybuddha.com/wis
    dom-quotes/fear-is-faith-that-it-wont-
    work-out/ Retrieved 6/09/2020.
10. Unknown. https://tinybuddha.com/wis
    dom-quotes/many-flaws-perfect-many-
    blessings-ungrateful/
    Retrieved 6/09/2020.
11. Neil Armstrong. https://
    www.brainyquote.com/quotes/neil_arm
    strong_135030 Retrieve 6/09/2020.
12. Dhammapda. https://tinybuddha.com/
    wisdom-quotes/do-not-give-your-attent
    ion-to-what-others-do-or-fail-to-do-give-
    it-to-what-you-do-or-fail-to-do/
    Retrieved 6/07/2020.
13. John Burroughs.https://
    www.brainyquote.com/quotes/john_bur
    roughs_120946 Retrieve 6/09/2020.
14. Mahatma Gandhi. https://tinybuddha.
    com/wisdom-quotes/our-greatness-lies-
    not-so-much-in-being-able-to-remake-t
    he-world-as-being-able-to-remake-our
    selves/ Retrieved 6/09/2020.
15. Albert Einstein. https://
    www.brainyquote.com/quotes/albert_e
    instein_118979 Retrieved 6/07/2020.

References

16.   Charles H. Spurgeon. https://www.
goodreads.com/quotes/29559-wisdom-
is-the-right-use-of-knowledge-to-know-is
Retrieved 6/07/2020.

17.   Paulo Coelho. https://www.goodreads.
com/quotes/730518-if-it-s-still-in-your-
mind-it-is-worth-taking
Retrieved 6/09/2020.

18.   Mandy Hale.https://www.goodreads.
com/quotes/7140087-you-don-t-always-
need-a-plan-sometimes-you-just-need
Retrieved 06/10/2020.

19.   Epictetus.https://www.brainyquote.com/
quotes/epictetus_384552
Retrieved 06/10/2020.

20.   Brian Tracy.https://tinybuddha.com/wis
dom-quotes/you-can-only-grow-if-you-
re-willing-to-feel-awkward-and-uncom
fortable-when-you-try-something-new/
Retrieved 06/10/2020.

21.   Ralph Waldo Emerson. https://tinybud
dha.com/wisdom-quotes/our-strength-
grows-out-of-our-weaknesses/
Retrieved 06/10/2020.

22.   Unknown.https://tinybuddha.com/wis
dom-quotes/choose-see-good-others-
end-finding-good/
Retrieved 06/10/2020.

References

23. Unknown. https://tinybuddha.com/wis
dom-quotes/focus-loving-instead-loving-
idea-people-loving/
Retrieved 06/10/2020.

24. Unknown. https://tinybuddha.com/wis
dom-quotes/the-best-way-to-keep-good-
intention-from-dying-is-to-execute-them
Retrieved 06/10/2020.

25. Natalie Babbitt. https://tinybuddha.com/
wisdom-quotes/dont-be-afraid-of-death-
be-afraid-of-an-unlived-life-you-dont-
have-to-live-forever-you-just-have-to-
live/ Retrieved 06/10/2020.

26. Morrie Schwartz. https://tinybuddha.
com/wisdom-quotes/the-most-important-
thing-in-this-world-is-to-learn-to-give-
out-love-and-let-it-come-in/
Retrieved 06/10/2020.

27 Sir Edmund Hillary. https://
www.brainyquote.com/quotes/ed
mund_hillary_104652
Retrieved 06/10/2020.

28. Unknown. http://www.changeforhealth.
com/a-community-of-people/
Retrieved 06/10/2020.

29. Dr. David Schwartz. https://tinybuddha.
com/wisdom-quotes/when-you-believe-
something-can-be-done-really-believe-
your-mind-will-find-ways-to-do-it/
Retrieved 06/10/2020.

References

30.   Raymond Hull. https://
     www.brainyquote.com/quotes/ray
     mond_hull_104270
     Retrieved 06/10/2020.

31.   Eleanor Roosevelt. https://
     www.brainyquote.com/quotes/
     eleanor_roosevelt_143006
     Retrieved 06/11/2020.

32.   Mark Twain. https://www.goodreads.
     com/quotes/219455-the-secret-of-get
     ting-ahead-is-getting-started-the-secret
     Retrieved 06/07/2020.

33.   Napoleon Hill. https://www.brainyquote.
     com/quotes/napoleon_hill_152843
     Retrieved 06/11/2020.

34.   John Bradshaw. https://
     www.brainyquote.com/quotes/
     john_bradshaw_133988
     Retrieved 06/11/2020.

35.   Aesop. https://www.brainyquote.com/
     quotes/aesop_382596
     Retrieved 06/11/2020.

36.   Ralph Waldo Emerson. https://
     www.brainyquote.com/quotes/
     ralph_waldo_emerson_106883
     Retrieved 06/11/2020.

References

37. Unknown. https://tinybuddha.com/wis dom-quotes/one-bad-chapter-doesnt-mean-your-storys-over/ Retrieved 06/11/2020.
38. Albert Einstein.https:// www.brainyquote.com/quotes/albert_e instein_174001 Retrieved 06/11/2020.
39. Michael Korda.https:// www.brainyquote.com/quotes/ michael_korda_135023 Retrieved 06/1120
40. Charles Buxton. https:// www.brainyquote.com/quotes/ charles_buxton_104418 Retrieved 06/11/2020.
41. Amelia Earhart. https:// www.brainyquote.com/quotes/ameli a_earhart_163002 Retrieved 06/11/2020.
42. Zig Ziglar. https://www.brainyquote.com/ quotes/zig_ziglar_617761 Retrieved 06/12/2020.
43. Joseph B. Wirthlin. https:// www.brainyquote.com/quotes/ joseph_b_wirthlin_645832 Retrieved 06/12/2020.

References

44.   Jim Rohn. https://www.brainyquote.com/
quotes/jim_rohn_165075
Retrieved 06/12/2020.

45.   African proverb. https://tinybuddha.com/
wisdom-quotes/when-there-is-no-ene
my-within-the-enemies-outside-cannot-
hurt-you-2/ Retrieved 06/12/2020.

46.   Paulo Coelho. https://tinybuddha.com/
wisdom-quotes/simple-things-also-ex
traordinary-things-wise-can-see/
Retrieved 06/13/2020.

47.   Lao Tzu. https://www.brainyquote.com/
quotes/lao_tzu_380274
Retrieved 06/13/2020.

48.   Unknown. http://www.changeforhealth.
com/doing-your-best/
Retrieved 06/13/2020.

49.   Winston Churchill. https://
www.brainyquote.com/quotes/win
ston_churchill_124653
Retrieved 06/13/2020.

50   Unknown. https://tinybuddha.com/wis
dom-quotes/let-whatever-today-enough/
Retrieved 06/13/2020.

51.   Og Mandino. https://www.brainyquote.
com/quotes/og_mandino_157857
Retrieved 06/13/2020.

References

52. George Lucas. https://www.brainyquote.com/quotes/george_lucas_462204
Retrieved 06/13/2020.

53. Unknown. https://tinybuddha.com/wisdom-quotes/okay-start-okay-rebuild-okay-scared/
Retrieved 06/13/2020.

54. Unknown. https://tinybuddha.com/wisdom-quotes/still-long-way-go-im-already-far-used-im-proud/
Retrieved 06/13/2020.

55. Ray Bradbury. https://www.brainyquote.com/quotes/ray_bradbury_447440
Retrieved 06/13/2020.

56. Unknown. https://tinybuddha.com/wisdom-quotes/regrets-just-lessons-worries-just-acceptance-expectations-just-gratitude-life-short
Retrieved 06/13/2020.

57. Unknown. https://tinybuddha.com/wisdom-quotes/secret-happy-accepting-life-making-every-dayRetrieved 06/13/2020.

58. Unknown. https://tinybuddha.com/wisdom-quotes/many-fine-things-can-be-done-in-a-day-if-you-don-t-always-make-that-day-tomorrow/
Retrieved 06/13/2020.

References

59.   Unknown. https://tinybuddha.com/wis
dom-quotes/stop-hating-everything-ar
ent-start-loving-everything/
Retrieved 06/13/2020.

60.   Beverly Sills. https://www.brainyquote.c
om/quotes/beverly_sills_101801
Retrieved 06/13/2020.

61.   Unknown. https://tinybuddha.com/wis
dom-quotes/every-new-day-is-another-
chance-to-change-your-life/
Retrieved 06/13/2020.

62.   Kahlil Gibran. https://www.goodreads.
com/quotes/892897-our-anxiety-does-
not-come-from-thinking-about-the-future
Retrieved 06/13/2020.

63.   Proverb. https://tinybuddha.com/wis
dom-quotes/grow-where-you-are-plant
ed/ Retrieved 06/13/2020.

64.   Unknown. https://tinybuddha.com/wis
dom-quotes/the-only-time-you-run-out-
of-chances-is-when-you-stop-taking-
them/ Retrieved 06/13/2020.

65.   C.S. Lewis. https://www.brainyquote.
com/quotes/c_s_lewis_119175
Retrieved 06/13/2020.

66.   Unknown. https://tinybuddha.com/wis
dom-quotes/we-are-limited-not-by-our-
abilities-but-by-our-vision/
Retrieved 06/13/2020.

References

67.   Unknown. https://tinybuddha.com/wis
       dom-quotes/value-doesnt-decrease-
       based-someones-inability-see-worth/
       Retrieved 06/13/2020.

68.   Milton Erickson. https://tinybuddha.com/
       wisdom-quotes/life-will-bring-you-pain-
       all-by-itself-your-responsibility-is-to-cre
       ate-joy/ Retrieved 06/13/2020.

69   Unknown.https://tinybuddha.com/wis
       dom-quotes/use-your-smile-to-change-
       the-world-dont-let-the-world-change-
       your-smile/ Retrieved 06/13/2020.

70.   Shirley Maclaine. https://tinybuddha.
       com/wisdom-quotes/dwelling-on-the-
       negative-simply-contributes-to-its-pow
       er/ Retrieved 06/13/2020.

71.   Stefan Sagmeister. https://www.
       goodreads.com/quotes/248815-com
       plaining-is-silly-either-act-or-forget
       Retrieved 06/13/2020.

72.   Robert Schuller. https://www.goodread
       s.com/book/show/1374307.Tough_
       Times_Never_Last_but_Tough_Peo
       ple_Do_ Retrieved 06/13/2020.

73.   Sam Levenson. https://
       www.brainyquote.com/quotes/
       sam_levenson_166055
       Retrieved 06/13/2020.

References

74. Fay Weldon.https://www.goodreads.
    com/quotes/7271907-if-you-do-nothing-
    unexpected-nothing-unexpected-hap
    pens Retrieved 06/13/2020.

75. Elbert Hubbard. https://quotefancy.com/
    quote/799614/Elbert-Hubbard-Don-t-
    make-excuses-make-good
    Retrieved 06/13/2020.

76. Confucius. https://www.goodreads.com/
    quotes/64564-the-man-who-moves-a-
    mountain-begins-by-carrying-away
    Retrieved 06/13/2020.

77. Dalai Lama. https://www.brainyquote.
    com/quotes/dalai_lama_166116
    Retrieved 06/13/2020.

78. William Arthur Ward. https://
    www.brainyquote.com/quotes/
    william_arthur_ward_100517
    Retrieved 06/13/2020.

79. **Gautama Buddha.** https://www.
    goodreads.com/quotes/751624-if-you-
    are-facing-in-the-right-direction-all-you
    Retrieved 06/13/2020.

80. Ennius. https://quotefancy.com/quote/
    892792/Quintus-Ennius-The-idle-mind-
    knows-not-what-it-wants
    Retrieved 06/13/2020.

References

81. Salvador Dali. https://www.brainyquote.
     com/quotes/salvador_dali_120513
     Retrieved 06/13/2020.
82. Will Smith. https://www.goodreads.com/
     quotes/937370-if-you-re-not-making-
     someone-else-s-life-better-then-you-re
     Retrieved 06/13/2020.
83. Gautama Buddha. https://
     www.brainyquote.com/quotes/bud
     dha_385920 Retrieved 06/13/2020.
84. Dalai Lama XIV. https://www.goodread
     too-small-to-make-a
     Retrieved 06/13/2020.
85. Napoleon Hill. https://www.goodreads.
     com/quotes/844847-if-you-do-not-con
     quer-self-you-will-be-conquered
     Retrieved 06/13/2020.
86. Eckhart Tolle.https://tinybuddha.com/
     wisdom-quotes/worry-pretends-neces
     sary-serves-no-useful-purpose/
     Retrieved 06/13/2020.
87. Lao Tzu, Tao Te Ching.https://www.
     goodreads.com/quotes/13843-a-man-
     with-outward-courage-dares-to-die-a-
     man Retrieved 06/13/2020.

References

88.   Robert Tew. https://tinybuddha.com/wis
        dom-quotes/struggle-youre-today-de
        veloping-strength-need-tomorrow-dont-
        give/ Retrieved 06/13/2020.
89.   Williams James. https://www.passiton.
        com/inspirational-quotes/4460-the-
        deepest-craving-of-human-nature-is-the-
        need Retrieved 06/13/2020.
90.   Henry Ford. https://www.quotes.net/
        quote/6037 Retrieved 06/13/2020.
91.   Anthony J. D'Angelo. https://
        www.brainyquote.com/quotes/antho
        ny_j_dangelo_153989
        Retrieved 06/14/2020.
92.   George Bernard Shaw. https://
        www.brainyquote.com/quotes/
        george_bernard_shaw_102967
        Retrieved 06/14/2020.
93.   Jim Rohn. https://www.brainyquote.com/
        quotes/jim_rohn_109882
        Retrieved 06/14/2020.
94.   Dave Checketts. https://tinybuddha.com/
        wisdom-quotes/success-builds-charac
        ter-failure-reveals-it/
        Retrieved 06/14/2020.
95.   Robert Brault. https://www.azquotes.
        com/quote/799902
        Retrieved 06/14/2020.

References

96.   Soren Kierkegaard. https:// www.brainyquote.com/quotes/ soren_kierkegaard_414008 Retrieved 06/14/2020.

97.   Proverb. https://tinybuddha.com/wis dom-quotes/all-the-flowers-of-all-the-tomorrows-are-in-the-seeds-of-today/ Retrieved 06/14/2020.

98.   Philippine Proverb. https://www.change forhealth.com/no-burnt-rice/ Retrieved 06/14/2020.

99.   Henri Frederic Amiel. https:// www.brainyquote.com/quotes/hen ri_frederic_amiel_104203 Retrieved 06/14/2020.

100.   Michael Jordan.https:// www.brainyquote.com/quotes/ michael_jordan_104651 Retrieved 06/14/2020.

101.   Buddhist Proverb. http://www.quotehd. com/quotes/buddhist-proverb-quote-when-the-student-is-ready-the-master-appears Retrieved 06/13/2020.

102.   Ken Robinson.https://www.goodreads. com/quotes/809838-curiosity-is-the-en gine-of-achievement Retrieved 06/14/2020.

References

103.   Richard Bach. https://www.brainyquote.
        com/quotes/richard_bach_149559
        Retrieved 06/14/2020.104.John F.
        Kennedy. https://
        www.brainyquote.com/quotes/
        john_f_kennedy_130001
        Retrieved 06/14/2020.
105.   William Hazlitt. https://www.goodreads.
        com/quotes/951147-the-more-we-do-
        the-more-we-can-do-the
        Retrieved 06/14/2020.
106.   Babe Ruth. https://www.brainyquote.
        com/quotes/babe_ruth_378138
        Retrieved 06/16/2020.
107.   Victor Kiam. https://www.brainyquote.
        com/quotes/victor_kiam_120741
        Retrieved 06/16/2020.
108.   Henry David Thoreau. https://
        www.brainyquote.com/quotes/henry_
        david_thoreau_106041
        Retrieved 06/16/2020.
109.   Maya Angelou. https://www.goodreads.
        com/quotes/7273813-do-the-best-you-
        can-until-you-know-better-then
        Retrieved 06/16/2020.

References

110. Unknown. https://tinybuddha.com/wis
dom-quotes/forget-all-the-reasons-it-
wont-work-and-believe-the-one-reason-
that-it-will/ Retrieved 06/14/2020.

111. Albert Einstein. https://
www.brainyquote.com/quotes/albert_e
instein_121643 Retrieved 06/14/2020.

112. Steve Maraboli. https://www.goodread
s.com/quotes/1152614-why-let-go-of-
yesterday-because-yesterday-has-al
ready-let Retrieved 06/17/2020.

113. Elizabeth Barrett Browning. https://
www.brainyquote.com/quotes/eliza
beth_barrett_brownin_163983
Retrieved 06/18/2020.

114. Tom Krause. https://tinybuddha.com/
wisdom-author/tom-krause/
Retrieved 06/21/2020.

115. Stephen Covey. https://
www.brainyquote.com/quotes/stephen_
covey_636539
Retrieved 06/21/2020.

116. Lao Tzu. https://www.brainyquote.com/
quotes/lao_tzu_379184
Retrieved 06/21/2020.

117. Max de Pree. https://www.brainyquote.
com/quotes/max_de_pree_377124
Retrieved 06/21/2020.

References

118. Scott Hamilton. https://
      www.brainyquote.com/quotes/scot
      t_hamilton_104173
      Retrieved 06/21/2020.
119. Mencius. https://www.brainyquote.com/
      quotes/mencius_379023
      Retrieved 06/21/2020.
120. George Bernard Shaw. https://
      www.brainyquote.com/quotes/
      george_bernard_shaw_109542
      Retrieved 06/21/2020.
121. Brian Tracy. https://www.brainyquote.
      com/quotes/brian_tracy_125848
      Retrieved 06/21/2020.
122. Robert H. Schuller. http://www.change
      forhealth.com/problems-are-guidelines/
      Retrieved 06/21/2020.
123. Carl Roger. https://www.goodreads.com/
      quotes/50836-the-curious-paradox-is-t
      hat-when-i-accept-myself-just
      Retrieved 06/21/2020.
124. Jesse Owens.https://www.brainyquote.
      com/quotes/jesse_owens_166163
      Retrieved 06/21/2020.

References

125. Unknown. https://tinybuddha.com/wis
      dom-quotes/above-all-be-true-to-your
      self-and-if-you-cannot-put-your-heart-in-
      it-take-yourself-out-of-it-2/
      Retrieved 06/21/2020.
126. Anatole France. https://
      www.brainyquote.com/quotes/ana
      tole_france_161340
      Retrieved 06/21/2020.
127. William James. https://
      www.brainyquote.com/quotes/william
      james_101061   Retrieved 06/21/2020.
128. Tom Robbins. https://tinybuddha.com/
      wisdom-quotes/stay-committed-in-your-
      decisions-but-stay-flexible-in-your-ap
      proach/ Retrieved 06/21/2020.
129. Celestine Chua. https://tinybuddha.com/
      wisdom-quotes/fear-uncertainty-and-
      discomfort-are-your-compasses-toward-
      growth/ Retrieved 06/21/2020.
130. Joni Eareckson Tada. https://
      www.brainyquote.com/quotes/j
      oni_eareckson_tada_526385
      Retrieved 06/21/2020.
131. Ziad K. Abdelnour. https://tinybuddha.
      com/wisdom-quotes/never-let-success-
      go-head-never-let-failure-go-heart/
      Retrieved 06/21/2020.

References

132. Zig Ziglar. https://www.brainyquote.com/
      quotes/zig_ziglar_132507
      Retrieved 06/21/2020.
133. Mike Dooley. https://tinybuddha.com/
      wisdom-quotes/lifes-not-expecting-hop
      ing-wishing-becoming/
      Retrieved 06/21/2020.
134. Benjamin Franklin. https://
      www.brainyquote.com/quotes/benjam
      in_franklin_138217
      Retrieved 06/21/2020.
135. Aeschylus. https://www.brainyquote.
      com/quotes/aeschylus_398833
      Retrieved 06/21/2020.
136. Socrates. https://www.brainyquote.com/
      quotes/socrates_380638
      Retrieved 06/21/2020.
137. Robert Tew. https://tinybuddha.com/wis
      dom-quotes/deny-ignore-delay-accept-
      face-conquer/ Retrieved 06/21/2020.
138. Anne Roiphe. https://www.brainyquote.
      com/quotes/anne_roiphe_575179
      Retrieved 06/21/2020.
139. Unknown. https://tinybuddha.com/wis
      dom-quotes/be-thankful-when-you-don-
      t-know-something-for-it-gives-you-the-
      opportunity-to-learn/
      Retrieved 06/21/2020.

References

140.   James Baldwin. https://www.goodread
s.com/quotes/14374-not-everything-
that-is-faced-can-be-changed-but-noth
ing Retrieved 06/21/2020.

141.   Buddha. https://www.goodreads.com/
quotes/16727-you-only-lose-what-you-
cling-to Retrieved 06/21/2020.

142.   Unknown. https://tinybuddha.com/wis
dom-quotes/commitment-in-the-face-of-
conflict-produces-character/
Retrieved 06/21/2020.

143.   Unknown. https://tinybuddha.com/wis
dom-quotes/still-long-way-go-im-al
ready-far-used-im-proud/
Retrieved 06/21/2020.

144.   Warren Buffett. https://
www.brainyquote.com/quotes/war
ren_buffett_409214

145.   Unknown. https://tinybuddha.com/wis
dom-quotes/regrets-just-lessons-wor
ries-just-acceptance-expectations-just-
gratitude-life-short/
Retrieved 06/21/2020.

146.   Robert Tew. https://www.goodreads.
com/quotes/7091872-the-person-who-
doesn-t-value-you-is-blocking-you-from
Retrieved 06/21/2020.

References

147.   Brian Tracy. https://tinybuddha.com/wis
dom-quotes/stress-unhappiness-come-
not-situations-respond-situations/
Retrieved 06/21/2020.

148.   Mandy Hale. https://tinybuddha.com/
wisdom-quotes/todays-a-good-day-to-
start-walking-in-the-opposite-direction-
of-anything-or-anyone-that-causes-you-
more-sorrow-than-joy/
Retrieved 06/21/2020.

149.   Lyndon B. Johnson. https://
www.brainyquote.com/quotes/lyn
don_b_johnson_103549
Retrieved 06/21/2020.

150.   Napoleon Hill. https://www.brainyquote.
com/quotes/napoleon_hill_152843
Retrieved 06/21/2020.

151.   Joyce Meyer. https://tinybuddha.com/
wisdom-quotes/dont-wait-everything-
perfect-decide-enjoy-life/
Retrieved 06/21/2020.

152.   Nelson Mandela. https://www.goodread
s.com/quotes/36606-it-always-seems-
impossible-until-it-s-done
Retrieved 06/21/2020.

153.   Peter Drucker. https://
www.brainyquote.com/quotes/peter
drucker_131600
Retrieved 06/21/2020.

References

154,   Albert Camus. https://www.goodreads.
com/quotes/626794-freedom-is-nothing-
else-but-a-chance-to-be-better
Retrieved 06/21/2020.

155.   George Sand. https://www.brainyquote.
com/quotes/george_sand_122325
Retrieved 06/21/2020.

156.   Unknown. https://tinybuddha.com/wis
dom-quotes/make-your-optimism-come-
true/ Retrieved 06/21/2020.

157.   Unknown. https://tinybuddha.com/wis
dom-quotes/sometimes-person-needs-
brilliant-mind-speaks-patient-heart-lis
tens/ Retrieved 06/21/2020.

158   Unknown. https://emilysquotes.com/al
ways-end-the-day-with-a-positive-
thought-no-matter-how-hard-things-
were-tomorrows-a-fresh-opportunity-to-
make-it-better/ Retrieved 06/21/2020.

159.   Vivian Greene. https://www.goodreads.
com/author/quotes/769264.Vivian_
Greene Retrieved 06/21/2020.

160.   F. Scott Fitzgerald.https://
www.brainyquote.com/quotes/f_scott_f
itzgerald_107068
Retrieved 06/21/2020.

References

161.   Martha Beck. https://www.brainyquote.
       com/quotes/martha_beck_282605
       Retrieved 06/21/2020.

162.   William Arthur Ward. https://
       www.brainyquote.com/quotes/
       william_arthur_ward_110017
       Retrieved 06/21/2020.

163.   Helmut Jahn. https://www.brainyquote.
       com/quotes/helmut_jahn_325255
       Retrieved 06/21/2020.

164.   Unknown. https://tinybuddha.com/wis
       dom-quotes/breathe-step-back-think-
       react-2/ Retrieved 06/21/2020.

165.   James R. Ball. https://www.goodreads.
       com/quotes/106610-we-cannot-achieve-
       more-in-life-than-what-we-believe

166.   Jean de la Gruyere. https://
       www.changeforhealth.com/out-of-diffi
       culties/ Retrieved 06/21/2020.

167.   Deepak Chopra. https://tinybuddha.com/
       wisdom-quotes/in-the-process-of-letting-
       go-you-will-lose-many-things-from-the-
       past-but-you-will-find-yourself/
       Retrieved 06/21/2020.

References

168.   Brigitte Nicole. https://tinybuddha.com/
       wisdom-quotes/never-define-relation
       ship-status-income-looks-generosity-
       kindness-compassion-counts/
       Retrieved 06/21/2020.

169.   Unknown. https://tinybuddha.com/wis
       dom-quotes/keep-your-head-clear-it-
       doesn-t-matter-how-bright-the-path-is-if-
       your-head-is-always-cloudy/
       Retrieved 06/21/2020.

170.   Unknown. https://tinybuddha.com/wis
       dom-quotes/you-can-do-what-s-reason
       able-or-you-can-decide-what-s-possible/
       Retrieved 06//21/2020.

171.   John Wooden. https://
       www.brainyquote.com/quotes/john_
       wooden_384233 Retrieved 06/21/2020.

172.   Dean Acheson. https://
       www.brainyquote.com/quotes/
       dean_acheson_132165
       Retrieved 06/21/2020.

173.   Laurence Sterne. https://
       www.brainyquote.com/quotes/lau
       rence_sterne_155708
       Retrieved 06/21/2020.

References

174. Soren Kierkegaard. https://
www.brainyquote.com/quotes/
soren_kierkegaard_105030
Retrieved 06/21/2020.
175. William James. https://
www.brainyquote.com/quotes/william_
james_385478 Retrieved 06/21/2020.
176. Dale Carnegie. https://
www.brainyquote.com/quotes/dale_
carnegie_386071
Retrieved 06/21/2020.
177. Fran Lebowitz. https://
www.brainyquote.com/quotes/fran_le
bowitz_102780
Retrieved 06/21/2020.
178. Unknown. https://tinybuddha.com/wis
dom-quotes/dont-afraid-take-unfamiliar-
path-sometimes-theyre-ones-take-best-
places/ Retrieved 06/21/2020.
179. Louise L. Hay. https://www.goodreads.
com/quotes/1316401-you-have-been-
criticizing-yourself-for-years-and-it-
hasn-t Retrieved 06/21/2020.
180. Helen Keller. https://www.brainyquote.
com/quotes/helen_keller_383771
Retrieved 06/21/2020.

References

181. Carl Jung. https://tinybuddha.com/wis dom-quotes/the-word-happiness-would-lose-its-meaning-if-it-were-not-balanced-by-sadness/ Retrieved 06/21/2020.

182. Denis Waitley. https://tinybuddha.com/ wisdom-quotes/you-must-welcome-change-as-the-rule-but-not-your-ruler/ Retrieved 06/21/2020.

183. Brian Tracy. https://tinybuddha.com/wis dom-quotes/set-peace-of-mind-as-your-highest-goal-and-organize-your-life-around-it/ Retrieved 06/21/2020.

184. Arthur C. Clarke. https:// www.brainyquote.com/quotes/ arthur_c_clarke_121735 Retrieved 06/21/2020.

185. Lao Tzu. https://www.brainyquote.com/ quotes/lao_tzu_137137 Retrieved 06/21/2020.

186. Gautama Buddha. https://www. goodreads.com/quotes/26838-your-pur pose-in-life-is-to-find-your-purpose-and Retrieved 06/21/2020.

References

187. Proverb. https://tinybuddha.com/wis
dom-quotes/a-good-plan-today-is-better-
than-a-perfect-plan-tomorrow/
Retrieved 06/2020.

188. Unknown. https://tinybuddha.com/wis
dom-quotes/the-grass-is-always-green
er-where-you-water-it/
Retrieved 06/2020.

189. Jimmy Dean. https://www.brainyquote.
com/quotes/jimmy_dean_131287
Retrieved 06/2020.

190. Rose Kennedy. https://
www.brainyquote.com/quotes/
rose_kennedy_134996

191. Will Rogers. https://www.goodreads.
com/quotes/23961-even-if-you-are-on-
the-right-track-you-ll-get
Retrieved 06/2020.

192 Lewis Carroll, Alice in Wonderland.
https://www.goodreads.com/quotes/
370441-i-could-tell-you-my-adventures-
beginning-from-this-morning-said
Retrieved 06/2020.

193. David Viscott. https://www.change
forhealth.com/your-self-respect-blos
soms/ Retrieved 06/2020

References

194. Peter Elbow. https://tinybuddha.com/ wisdom-quotes/meaning-is-not-what-you-start-with-but-what-you-end-up-with/ Retrieved 06/21/2020.

195. Hellen Keller. https://www.brainyquote. com/quotes/helen_keller_162480 Retrieved 06/21/2020.

196. Ray Bradbury. https://www.brainyquote. com/quotes/ray_bradbury_383404 Retrieved 06/21/2020.

197. Henry Wadsworth Longfellow. https:// www.brainyquote.com/quotes/hen ry_wadsworth_longfello_108465 Retrieved 06/21/2020.

198. Confucius. https://www.brainyquote. com/quotes/confucius_140908 Retrieved 06/21/2020.

199. Norman Vincent Peale. https:// www.brainyquote.com/quotes/nor man_vincent_peale_130593 Retrieved 06/21/2020.

200. Iyanla Vanzant. https://www.goodread s.com/quotes/39292-your-willingness-to-look-at-your-darkness-is-what-empow ers Retrieved 06/2020.

201. Terri Guillemets. https://www.wiseold sayings.com/authors/terri-guillemets-quotes/ Retrieved 06/2020.

References

202.   Jimmy Dean. https://www.brainyquote.
       com/quotes/jimmy_dean_412461
       Retrieved 06/2020

203.   George Santayana. https://
       www.brainyquote.com/quotes/
       george_santayana_382898
       Retrieved 06/21/2020.

204.   Franklin Roosevelt. https://
       www.brainyquote.com/quotes/
       franklin_d_roosevelt_101840
       Retrieved 06/21/2020.

205.   George Colman. https://
       www.brainyquote.com/quotes/george_
       colman_182722 Retrieved 06/21/2020.

206.   Philip Sidney. https://www.brainyquote.
       com/quotes/philip_sidney_160088
       Retrieved 06/21/2020.

207.   Unknown. http://www.quotss.com/quote/
       If-you-really-put-a-small-value-upon-
       yourself-rest-assured-that-the-world
       Retrieved 06/21/2020.

208.   Unknown.https://tinybuddha.com/wis
       dom-quotes/don-t-be-pushed-by-your-
       problems-be-led-by-your-dreams/
       Retrieved 06/21/2020.

209.   Lao Tzu. https://www.brainyquote.com/
       quotes/lao_tzu_383760
       Retrieved 06/21/2020.

References

210.   Unknown. https://tinybuddha.com/wis
       dom-quotes/dont-be-afraid-of-change-
       you-may-lose-something-good-but-you-
       may-gain-something-better/
       Retrieved 06/21/2020.

211.   Unknown. https://tinybuddha.com/wis
       dom-quotes/the-pain-you-feel-today-will-
       be-the-strength-you-feel-tomorrow/
       Retrieved 06/2020.

212.   Unknown. https://www.scrapbook.com/
       quotes/doc/12703.html
       Retrieved 06/2020

213.   Unknown. https://tinybuddha.com/wis
       dom-quotes/cant-start-next-chapter-life-
       keep-re-reading-last-one/
       Retrieved 06/2020

214.   W. Clement Stone. https://
       www.brainyquote.com/quotes/w_
       clement_stone_155728
       Retrieved 06/21/2020.

215.   Benjamin Disraeli. https://www.
       goodreads.com/quotes/38742-nurture-
       your-mind-with-great-thoughts-for-you-
       will-never Retrieved 06/21/2020.

References

216. Ellen Sue Stern. https://tinybuddha.
com/wisdom-quotes/believing-in-our-
hearts-that-who-we-are-is-enough-is-
the-key-to-a-more-satisfying-and-bal
anced-life/ Retrieved 06/21/2020.
217. Dalai Lama.https://www.goodreads.com/
quotes/125985-remember-that-some
times-not-getting-what-you-want-is-a
Retrieved 06/21/2020.
218. Hermann Hesse. https://tinybuddha.
com/wisdom-quotes/within-you-there-is-
a-stillness-and-a-sanctuary-to-which-
you-can-retreat-at-any-time-and-be-
yourself/ Retrieved 06/21/2020.
219. Alan Cohen.https://tinybuddha.com/wis
dom-quotes/do-not-wait-until-the-condi
tions-are-perfect-to-begin-beginning-
makes-the-conditions-perfect/
Retrieved 06/21/2020.
220. Unknown. https://tinybuddha.com/wis
dom-quotes/if-youre-not-willing-to-learn-
no-one-can-help-you-if-youre-deter
mined-to-learn-no-one-can-stop-you/
Retrieved 06/21/2020.
221. Marquis de Condorcet. https://
www.brainyquote.com/quotes/mar
quis_de_condorcet_305860
Retrieved 06/21/2020.

References

222. Charles Atlas. https://www.brainyquote.com/quotes/charles_atlas_179487 Retrieved 06/21/2020.

223. Andrew Ryan. https://www.goodreads.com/quotes/669319-we-all-make-choices-but-in-the-end-our-choices Retrieved 06/21/2020.

224. Warren Buffett. https://www.brainyquote.com/quotes/warren_buffett_138173 Retrieved 06/21/2020

225. Malcolm S. Forbes. https://www.brainyquote.com/quotes/malcolm_forbes_102078 Retrieved 06/21/2020.

226 Leo Buscaglia. https://www.brainyquote.com/quotes/leo_buscaglia_108583 Retrieved 06/21/2020.

227. Churchill. https://www.brainyquote.com/quotes/winston_churchill_125996 Retrieved 06/21/2020.

228. Dr. Seuss. https://www.passiton.com/inspirational-quotes/6639-sometimes-you-will-never-know-the-value-of-a Retrieved 06/22/2020.

229. James Allen.https://www.brainyquote.com/quotes/james_allen_133802 Retrieved 06/22/2020.

References

230.   Unknown. https://tinybuddha.com/wis
        dom-quotes/always-concentrate-on-
        how-far-you-ve-come-rather-than-how-
        far-you-have-left-to-go/
        Retrieved 06/22/2020.
231.   Caroline Myss. https://tinybuddha.com/
        wisdom-quotes/not-seek-need-approval-
        powerful/ Retrieved 06/22/2020.
232.   Vironika Tugaleva. https://www.
        goodreads.com/quotes/6107308-you-ll-
        never-know-who-you-are-unless-you-
        shed-who Retrieved 06/22/2020.
233.   Unknown. https://tinybuddha.com/wis
        dom-quotes/let-go-of-the-need-to-con
        trol-the-outcome-trust-the-process-trust-
        your-intuition-trust-yourself/
        Retrieved 06/22/2020.
234.   Michael John Bobak. https://www.
        goodreads.com/quotes/6999386-all-
        progress-takes-place-outside-the-com
        fort-zone Retrieved 06/22/2020.
235.   Norman Vincent Peale. https://www.
        goodreads.com/quotes/531570-live-
        your-life-and-forget-your-age
        Retrieved 06/22/2020.

References

236. Unknown. https://www.change forhealth.com/people-who-believe-in-themselves/ Retrieved 06/21/2020.

237. Robert Frost. https://www.brainyquote. com/quotes/robert_frost_101059 Retrieved 06/22/2020.

238. Carol Burnett. https://www.brainyquote. com/quotes/carol_burnett_371189 Retrieved 06/22/2020.

239. Buddha. https://www.goodreads.com/ quotes/81713-every-morning-we-are-born-again-what-we-do-today Retrieved 06/22/2020.

240. Thomas Edison. https://www.goodread s.com/quotes/8582119-never-go-to-sleep-without-a-request-to-your-subcon scious Retrieved 06/22/2020.

241. Edward Eggleston. https://quotefancy. com/quote/757808/Edward-Eggleston-Persistent-people-begin-their-success-where-others-end-in-failure Retrieved 06/22/2020.

242. Oscar Wilde. https://www.goodreads. com/quotes/2020.1557-what-seems-to-us-as-bitter-trials-are-often-blessings Retrieved 06/22/2020.

243. Paul Valéry. https://www.brainyquote. com/quotes/paul_valery_121250 Retrieved 06/22/2020.

References

244. Albert Einstein. https://www.brainyquote.com/quotes/albert_einstein_122232 Retrieved 06/22/2020.

245. Eckhart Tolle. https://tinybuddha.com/wisdom-quotes/surrender-say-yes-life-see-life-suddenly-starts-working-rather/ Retrieved 06/22/2020.

246. Mahatma Gandhi. https://tinybuddha.com/wisdom-quotes/an-ounce-of-practice-is-worth-tons-of-preaching/ Retrieved 06/22/2020.

247. Abraham H. Maslow. https://tinybuddha.com/wisdom-quotes/every-really-new-idea-looks-crazy-first/ Retrieved 06/22/2020.

248. Robin Sharma. https://tinybuddha.com/wisdom-quotes/beautiful-thing-setbacks-introduce-us-strengths/ Retrieved 06/23/2020.

249. Aristotle. https://www.goodreads.com/quotes/1003359-we-are-what-we-repeatedly-do-excellence-then-is-not Retrieved 06/23/2020.

250. Osho. https://tinybuddha.com/wisdom-quotes/get-out-of-your-head-and-get-into-your-heart-think-less-feel-more/ Retrieved 06/23/2020.

References

251. Johann Wolfgang von Goethe. https://www.goodreads.com/quotes/18941-as-soon-as-you-trust-yourself-you-will-know-how Retrieved 06/23/2020.

252. Helen Keller. https://www.quotes.net/quote/38616 Retrieved 06/23/2020.

253. Donald Miller. https://tinybuddha.com/wisdom-quotes/when-you-stop-expecting-people-to-be-perfect-you-can-like-them-for-who-they-are/ Retrieved 06/23/2020.

254. Peter F. Drucker. https://www.goodreads.com/quotes/420819-if-you-want-something-new-you-have-to-stop-doing Retrieved 06/23/2020.

255. Gerry Spence. https://tinybuddha.com/wisdom-quotes/i-would-rather-have-a-mind-opened-by-wonder-than-one-closed-by-belief/ Retrieved 06/23/2020.

256. Khalil. https://www.goodreads.com/quotes/5767-beauty-is-not-in-the-face-beauty-is-a-light Retrieved 06/23/2020.

257. Coleman Cox. https://www.goodreads.com/quotes/9353122-i-am-a-great-believer-in-luck-the-harder-i Retrieved 06/23/2020.

References

258.   William Penn. https://www.brainyquote.
        com/quotes/william_penn_107902
        Retrieved 06/23/2020.
259.   Jim Rohn. https://www.goodreads.com/
        quotes/7153428-everyone-must-
        choose-one-of-two-pains-the-pain-of
        Retrieved 06/23/2020.
260.   Napoleon. https://www.goodreads.com/
        quotes/130565-ability-is-of-little-ac
        count-without-opportunity
        Retrieved 06/23/2020.
261.   Buddha. https://www.treasurequotes.
        com/quotes/our-sorrows-and-wounds-
        are-healed-only-when-we
        Retrieved 06/23/2020.
262.   T. S. Eliot. https://www.brainyquote.com/
        quotes/t_s_eliot_161137
        Retrieved 06/23/2020.
263.   Jewish Proverb. https://www.goodread
        s.com/quotes/265178-i-ask-not-for-a-l
        ighter-burden-but-for-broader
        Retrieved 06/23/2020.
264.   Noam Chomsky. https://
        www.brainyquote.com/quotes/noam_
        chomsky_635694
        Retrieved 06/23/2020.

References

265. Frank A. Clark. https://www.brainyquote.com/quotes/frank_a_clark_156704
      Retrieved 06/23/2020.

266. Malcolm S. Forbes. https://www.brainyquote.com/quotes/malcolm_forbes_105931
      Retrieved 06/23/2020.

267. Doug Henning. https://quotefancy.com/quote/1641211/Doug-Henning-The-hard-must-become-habit-The-habit-must-become-easy-The-easy-must-become Retrieved 06/23/2020.

268. Richard Wilkins. https://tinybuddha.com/wisdom-quotes/miracles-start-happen-give-much-energy-dreams-fears/
      Retrieved 06/23/2020.

269. Paulo Coelho. https://www.goodreads.com/quotes/730518-if-it-s-still-in-your-mind-it-is-worth-taking
      Retrieved 06/23/2020.

270. Carl Jung. https://www.goodreads.com/quotes/50795-i-am-not-what-happened-to-me-i-am-what
      Retrieved 06/23/2020.

271. Jean Vanier. https://www.brainyquote.com/quotes/jean_vanier_201866
      Retrieved 06/23/2020.

References

272.   Unknown. https://tinybuddha.com/wis
dom-quotes/stop-afraid-go-wrong-focus-
go-right/ Retrieved 06/23/2020.

273.   Michelle C. Ustaszeski. https://tinybud
dha.com/quotes/tiny-wisdom-the-ideal-
time-to-appreciate-each-other/

274.   Johann Wolfgang von Goethe. https://
www.brainyquote.com/quotes/johann_
wolfgang_von_goeth_150574
Retrieved 06/23/2020.

275.   Unknown. https://tinybuddha.com/wis
dom-quotes/don-t-let-today-s-disap
pointments-cast-a-shadow-on-tomor
row-s-dreams/ Retrieved 06/23/2020.

276.   Henry David Thoreau. https://tinybud
dha.com/wisdom-quotes/i-cannot-make-
my-days-longer-so-i-strive-to-make-
them-better/ Retrieved 06/23/2020.

277.   Maria Robinson. https://www.goodread
s.com/quotes/186119-nobody-can-go-
back-and-start-a-new-beginning-but
Retrieved 06/23/2020.

278   Edgar Allen Poe. https://www.goodread
s.com/quotes/40870-never-to-suffer-
would-never-to-have-been-blessed
Retrieved 06/23/2020.

References

279. Aesop. https://www.goodreads.com/
quotes/16664-no-act-of-kindness-no-
matter-how-small-is-ever
Retrieved 06/23/2020.

280. Winston Churchill.https://
www.brainyquote.com/quotes/win
ston_churchill_131192
Retrieved 06/23/2020.

281. Ashley Hodgeson. https://tinybuddha.
com/wisdom-quotes/strongest-people-
arent-always-people-win-people-dont-
give-lose/ Retrieved 06/23/2020.

282. Martin Luther. https://www.goodreads.
com/author/show/29874.Martin_Luther
Retrieved 06/23/2020.

283. Dalai Lama. https://tinybuddha.com/wis
dom-quotes/see-the-positive-side-the-
potential-and-make-an-effort/
Retrieved 06/23/2020.

284. Proverb.https://tinybuddha.com/wisdom-
quotes/cheerfulness-is-the-best-promot
er-of-health/ Retrieved 06/23/2020.

285. Epictetus. https://quotefancy.com/quote/
802200/Epictetus-He-who-laughs-at-
himself-never-runs-out-of-things-to-
laugh-at Retrieved 06/23/2020.

References

286.   Unknown. https://tinybuddha.com/wis
dom-quotes/lifes-problems-wouldnt-
called-hurdles-wasnt-way-get/
Retrieved 06/23/2020.

287.   Buddha. https://tinybuddha.com/wis
dom-quotes/light-lamp-someone-else-
will-also-brighten-path/
Retrieved 06/23/2020.

288.   Plutarch. https://tinybuddha.com/wis
dom-quotes/the-whole-life-of-a-man-is-
but-a-point-in-time-let-us-enjoy-it/
Retrieved 06/23/2020.

289.   Jim Henson. https://www.goodreads.
com/quotes/476550-life-s-like-a-movie-
write-your-own-ending-keep-believing
Retrieved 06/23/2020.

290.   **Jawaharlal Nehru. https://
www.brainyquote.com/quotes/jawahar
lal_nehru_132485
Retrieved 06/23/2020.**

291.   Mother Teresa. https://tinybuddha.com/
wisdom-quotes/people-come-life-bless
ings-others-come-life-lessons/
Retrieved 06/23/2020.

292.   Benjamin Franklin. https://
www.brainyquote.com/quotes/benjam
in_franklin_104457
Retrieved 06/23/2020.

References

293.   Maya Angelou. https://www.goodreads.
com/quotes/700564-if-you-are-always-
trying-to-be-normal-you-will
Retrieved 06/23/2020

294.   Byron Katie. https://tinybuddha.com/
wisdom-quotes/taking-responsibility-for-
your-beliefs-and-judgments-gives-you-t
he-power-to-change-them/
Retrieved 06/23/2020.

295.   Unknown. https://tinybuddha.com/wis
dom-quotes/love-is-just-a-word-until-
someone-comes-along-and-gives-it-
meaning/ Retrieved 06/23/2020.

296.   Ursula K. Le Guin. https://www.
goodreads.com/quotes/44719-it-is-
good-to-have-an-end-to-journey-toward
Retrieved 06/23/2020.

297.   Lama Yeshe. https://tinybuddha.com/
wisdom-quotes/be-gentle-first-with-
yourself-if-you-wish-to-be-gentle-with-
others/ Retrieved 06/23/2020.

298.   Michael Altshuler. https://tinybuddha.
com/wisdom-quotes/the-bad-news-is-
time-flies-the-good-news-is-you-re-the-
pilot/ Retrieved 06/07/2020.

References

299.   Buddha. https://tinybuddha.com/wis
        dom-quotes/our-sorrows-and-wounds-
        are-healed-only-when-we-touch-them-
        with-compassion/
        Retrieved 6/07/2020.
300.   Albert Einstein https://
        www.brainyquote.com/quotes/albert_e
        instein_151946 Retrieved 6//07/30.
301.   Unknown Author.https://tinybuddha.com/
        wisdom-quotes/what-you-do-today-is-
        important-because-you-are-exchanging-
        a-day-of-your-life-for-it/
        Retrieved 6/07/2020.

About the Author

M. Eugene Morgan has been an avid student of Milton Erickson's work since 1993. He received his Associates Degrees in Behavioral Sciences/ Psychology and Liberal Arts in 1994 at San Diego Community College. In 1995, he received a certificate in hypnotherapy from the American Council of Hypnotist Examiners in San Diego, CA, an interest that ties in with his interest in Dr. Erickson's work. From 1996 to1998 he has provided free hypnotherapy to clients with HIV/AIDS at the San Diego Lesbian, Gay, Bisexual, and Transgender Community Center.

*S*ince 1999, he has had years of exposure to the persons-served community as an administrative assistant and now as a call center representative in the Mercy Crisis Center at Mercy Behavioral Health an outpatient mental health, drug and alcohol in Pittsburgh, PA, interacting with the persons-served, therapists, nurses, doctors, and case managers. Eugene is an author of two books Volume I and II of the Change For Health series now in paperback and Kindle version on Amazon.

www.ingramcontent.com/pod-product-compliance
Lightning Source LLC
Chambersburg PA
CBHW020601270326
41927CB00005B/118